SECRETS FROM THE FIELD

AN ETHNOGRAPHER'S NOTES FROM NORTH WESTERN PAKISTAN

By

BENEDICTE GRIMA

authorHOUSE™

1663 LIBERTY DRIVE, SUITE 200
BLOOMINGTON, INDIANA 47403
(800) 839-8640
WWW.AUTHORHOUSE.COM

© 2004 BENEDICTE GRIMA
All Rights Reserved.

First published by AuthorHouse 11/09/04

ISBN: 1-4208-0674-2 (sc)

Printed in the United States of America
Bloomington, Indiana

This book is printed on acid-free paper.

CONTENTS

INTRODUCTION

Ever since I have been involved with travel or fieldwork in the Muslim world of Iran, Afghanistan and northwest Pakistan, curious friends and colleagues have always asked what it was like to be a foreign woman on my own there. Later, when I spent eighteen months living in Pakistan's NWFP with my infant daughter, the curiosity doubled. And more recently, as suspicions have risen as to the possibility of Osama Bin Laden and other Al-Qaeda and Taliban leaders being exiled in the area, suspicions have tripled. What is that area like? What are the people like? What is it like for an outsider in this self-ruled tribal region forbidden to any outside government authority?

Any social scientist, and for that matter, anyone having ever undertaken work in a foreign culture, has made blunders, cultural mistakes which have accentuated their existence within that culture as laughable and anomalous, and which have taught them a valid lesson in that culture. The following are accounts of personal events, many of them blunders which I can now laugh at from a safe distance, but which at the time opened my eyes to things I should or should not do to not only exist within this culture, but to operate effectively in order to perform my task, that of participant observer.

Pashto, as has been illustrated by myself and others in length, is not just a language but a complex conglomerate of cultural behavior. One does not merely speak, but one does, one performs, Pashto. As my own linguistic skills grew, so did the behavioral expectations the culture had of me. When I first traveled to the area and my language was weak, I could act, dress, eat, travel, in short, behave as a foreigner. I could socialize with men, for instance, and all my behavior was tolerated. Each time I returned speaking better, I was slowly excluded from the male world and relegated to the female one. Attitudes toward my lack of adherence to ways of traveling, dressing and other behavior were increasingly unforgiving. The experience in the shrine is a good example of this, being taken from the end of my twelve year time.

The entire field work was conducted in the area bordering Afghanistan and North West Pakistan over a period of twelve years. I first drove in 1979 from Paris, France, where I was studying languages, remained two months in Yazd, Iran, two months in Afghanistan traveling, and two weeks in the Swat Valley of northwestern Pakistan. I was arrested in northern Afghanistan at a very tumultuous time in that country's history, and was turned out after ten days of house arrest. Iran was at this time (December, 1979) undergoing its own revolution, and I carefully kept to small back roads to cross that country to Turkey and back to Europe. That was the last I saw of Iran, and I was not to reenter Afghanistan for another decade.

During the 1980s, at the time of the Russian occupation of Afghanistan, I spent fifteen months based in Peshawar as the guest of Colonel Sherif and his wife, although from there I traveled extensively throughout the NWFP. I had then completed my M.A. from the University of Paris in Iranian Studies, where I studied Farsi, Pashto, Arabic and Urdu at the Langues Orientales. In the later 1980s, I again spent eighteen months with my daughter, Lawangina, in the NWFP, this time renting my own house in Peshawar to serve as a base. This I did with a Fulbright Hays Fellowship for doctoral research. From Peshawar, I also rented accommodations in Madyan, a tourist village in the Swat Valley for six months, and in Ahmadi Banda, a little known Khattak village for six months. This was the decisive research for my dissertation and book, *THE PERFORMANCE OF EMOTION AMONG PAXTUN WOMEN*. I did return to Afghanistan after the Russian withdrawal for some research on rural medical facilities and their accessibility to women.

The research resulting from all this has been published in many forms. But the accounts that follow are taken from field notes and journals which always accompanied me. Unlike academic writing, these are subjective accounts of personal events, and my own experiences of the culture I lived and studied. They are stories of people as I knew them, as experienced through my relationships with them. It is these events and experiences which taught me how to live there, showing me through my own mistakes where I was wrong and where successful.

These tales, taken entirely from field notes, are intended in answer to all those who have asked what it was like to travel and live as a woman on my own in this part of the world. Most of the experiences could be repeated today. Although there are obvious political changes, urban development in the area of Peshawar, and the refugee population has in large part been assimilated into Pakistan or gone home, the base cultural norms and beliefs remain the same.

Fortress in the Khyber

I. SAYYED – THE LIFE OF AN OUTLAW

Sayyed was a good citizen, a Sunite descendant of the caliph Ali. He was father to five children, resident of Kohat, and had served almost eighteen years as a skilled technician in the Pakistan army when one day, driven by passion in an argument over land, he happened to shoot and kill two members of his agnate family. As he was just three miles from the tribal territory where the police have no authority and could not hunt him down, he fled for refuge among the Pashtun tribes, where he made his way up to Dogal Khel, the fortress of his friend, a wealthy drug dealer of Landi Kotal near the Khyber Pass, who helped Sayyed escape to Europe.

For five years, Sayyed roamed and worked throughout the world. He worked on a Greek merchant ship for three years, filling his passport with visas from all over Europe, Russia and the United States. In Washington, he was issued a world passport by the U.N.O., but it was not recognized when he requested an immigration visa for the U.S. So, he went to London to work for two years, and when he was offered to remain there, he refused, thinking he could return and rectify things at home, and reunite with his family.

One day, after his five-year absence and without any warning, he returned to Pakistan with a suitcase full of money he had acquired. He flew straight to Peshawar and quickly took hidden refuge in the Afridi fortress of Dogal Khel again. I had met him on the plane, and agreed to come visit him there. Sayyed's brother was attempting to arrange a reconciliation with his cousins. If all went well, he could return home, reintegrate himself in the army with a pardon and pension, and resume as a trained technician. If not, he would once again leave his homeland and family, roaming and working wherever he could, trying to settle his graying head and slouching body somewhere permanently. And his sons, the next generation, would also be tracked and haunted, for these feuds get passed on in this way. Meanwhile, when I went to visit him the first time, he was still a man without a home, an eternal guest.

I asked him if the government police forces, knowing he was here, could not arrest one of his host's sons one day when they were in Peshawar, but he seemed not the least frightened. "If one man accepts you here, the whole tribal area accepts you, and if the government even attempts to interfere, the entire Afridi belt would stand up and fight to defend this one man and his protected guest. Accepting a man in your home, by Pashtun tribal law, implies guaranteeing the safety of his life, at the risk of your own."

Sayyed's cousins, as it turned out, did not accept any kind of reconciliation, and so, Sayyed, rather than flee the country again, he decided to settle in the tribal area. I went often to visit him, usually by sending word ahead of time. He would then send one of Haji's sons in a hired pick-up to get me from the city and escort me to the fortress. Once, in January of 1983, I was just getting home at the end of the day when someone handed me a message, hand-delivered from Jamrud: "Please come with Latif Khan. I am expecting you. Sayyed."

Although I had never heard of this Latif Khan, I knew exactly what I had to do, and did it. I had tea and fruit sent to him while I ran to change my clothes and fold up my work, stuffing just my shawl, a notebook, and some money in my plastic basket. Then I wrapped up in my long black veil, which I did not use inside the city. I announced to my host that I was off to Jamrud and would probably return the following day.

Latif Khan, a young thin boy of sixteen or seventeen, was patiently waiting in the garage, wrapped in a blanket. I thought he had come by car or pick-up, but he was on foot, so we left to catch the bus. A wind had begun blowing. It was one of the winter gales known to rage through the Peshawar Valley in winter, blowing dust in blinding vortices across the fields. The air had turned brown and the Khyber mountains separating Pakistan and Afghanistan had been swallowed up inside. Latif Khan didn't speak to me at all, only answering my questions with utmost deference. Mostly, I wanted to know why we were going to Jamrud rather than Landi Kotal to see Sayyed. Apparently, he had moved.

4

There had been heavy fighting in the Khyber during the last month between the Afridi and Shinwari tribes. The government was on a rampage to control the drug traffic originating in that area, and the tribes could not agree as to what measures to take. Several people had been reported killed over the disputes, and the area was officially closed off. So I wondered as I looked out my window, who sat in all the buses on the road. There were no road checks, and even I slipped by unnoticed into the area.

Latif Khan remained respectfully distant from me, ashamed to look at or speak with me, forced to sit next to me, but with his legs in the isle, and his back turned to me. A man can be arrested in Pakistan for being seen in any kind of relationship with an unrelated woman. But I was contemplating the disadvantage of being so respected. No one would talk to me. And as soon as most of the passengers, that is, Afghans climbed off at the large refugee camp at Board, he moved to another seat entirely. I kept my face turned to the window, my veil especially drawn, down over my eyes up over my nose, holding it tightly shut from underneath so that even my hand should not be seen. At no cost did I want to cause any trouble for myself or for Latif Khan for whom, I later discovered, the trip had been equally dangerous.

When the bus stopped for evening prayers, I noticed the poplar trees were bent over with the wind, which had by now gained considerable strength. It was dark by the time we arrived in Jamrud, and I quietly followed my escort to a shop, where he left me at a distance to squat unnoticed under my veil while he went to hire us a pick-up. Only once we were inside the vehicle did the young man begin to talk to me more openly, and did I loosen the grip on my veil. We were "home," so to speak. That's when he told me his own story.

Latif Khan was from Tirah, the tribal mountains just south of the Khyber. He had come to Kamal Khan's fortress for protection to escape fighting between his own and another clan. It had all started over wood. Someone had cut some trees for firewood on a particular mountain, and this aroused anger, for it was not their mountain, and the owners were demanding payment for the theft. This was refused, so the owners kidnapped four men from the wood-stealing family and held them tied up as hostages. The others then retaliated by trying to kidnap some of THEIR men as hostages, but shooting broke out, and one man was wounded. It would continue this way for some time, so, meanwhile, Latif Khan and a few other members of the family came to seek hospitality and protection from Kamal Khan. But, as he indicated to me, he feared his enemies at every moment, and wouldn't venture anywhere without his pistol and cartridge belt over his shoulder, which he had been obliged to leave behind to leave the tribal area and enter Peshawar to get me. I was slowly getting accustomed to having armed men surround me, and sleeping with a rifle within arm's reach.

Upon reaching the mud fort, which at once appeared less wealthy than Haji Nawab's in Landi Kotal, I was immediately ushered into the women's rooms. These were Afridis, wearing a different style of dress than I had yet seen, and speaking in very different accents, which took me a while, with head spinning, to understand. I was delighted, however, and felt very chatty after such a silent ride. There was little formality as we sat on cardboard around a lantern in the dark mud room. Latif soon came to bring me across the pitch black and very windy courtyard to a spare room, where Sayyed was expecting me. And there we sat and talked late into the night. Latif remained sitting on the floor and didn't utter a word. He had been designated as Sayyed's younger brother, therefore entirely disposed to serve him in any way.

Sayyed explained that he felt uncomfortable living as an eternal guest in Jamrud, and that Kamal Khan had offered him a plot here on which to build his own house. He wanted my advice on the design. I told him, based on what I had observed in my travels through different parts of the Northwest Frontier, that I thought mud would not only be cheaper, but would serve as better insolation than concrete. He asked me to draw a plan for his house. Why me? I put together my knowledge of appropriate architecture, taking into account the social and cultural exigencies, and drew something. But I asked if I could actually take part in the labor, as it would give me a chance to learn how the materials were used, as well as it would give me an excuse to remain some time in the area and work on my Afridi, as I suspected I would spend most of my social time with the women.

In effect, after our conversation, I rejoined Kamal Khan's wife, Ulicha, and their daughters, back in the inner house. Ulicha was originally from Tirah, so I asked her which place she preferred. "There's no wood here," she answered, "and there's the problem of water." In these stark, naked mountains there is no growth of any sort, except the occasional thorn bush, and wood is bought from the bazaar at expensive rates, which means it becomes a luxury item and is relegated to limited usage. But I teased her because this also meant less work for her. Fetching wood is traditionally a woman's chore, and a hard one. But now that it was bought from the bazaar, it had become a man's job. We all laughed over that.

We only stepped out into the courtyard to pee, and upon seeing the sky filled with more stars than I'd even seen, I wanted to bundle up in a blanket and take a long walk. Out of the question, naturally! The two young daughters slept in the room with me, both sharing the second cot and quilt. My quilt was so heavy with cotton that my legs ached from the

Man at his hearth.

weight over them. All night the wind howled against the loosely fitted wooden door, and strong drafts shook everything in the room. Still, it felt warm and very cosy. In the morning, we crossed the courtyard over to the main room for tea. This is where the women and I spent most of our time. There was no furniture, so we squatted around the wood fire in this room, used simultaneously as goat shed and kitchen. The other room housed the cots and trunks.

Sayyed and Latif took me for a walk in the lower hills, where we visited his plot. It was a large walled-in square belonging to Kamal Khan, in which he had already granted a part to some Shinwari Afghans three years ago, who had built their three rooms. Sayyed was getting the southern half, and was only going to take half of that, which would still give him space for three rooms, a kitchen and a large courtyard with a proper flush

7

latrine and shower at one end. He announced that one room would be mine, and I felt honored.

Meanwhile, however, Sayyed wanted me to go to Kohat, meet his wife and children and bring them news from him. This would have to be done with great discretion, as he did not want any of his in-laws knowing of his return or whereabouts in Pakistan. I began by locating Sayyed's sister, Malika, living with her husband on the outskirts of Peshawar. Also living with them was Sayyed's oldest son, Daud, whom I stay in touch with to this day. He was studying appliance technology and electrical engineering. It was a Hindko-speaking household, and I felt stifled by the language barrier. They stressed upon me the importance of not mentioning Sayyed's name under any circumstances when they took me to Kohat to meet the family, as no one knew of his whereabouts, and his enemies would be sure to ask me.

Daud, Malika and I took the bus to Kohat and began our visits, first to her in-laws, where we spent the day with all the women, going for a Friday walk to the family orchards. Our little group wound through the mud alleyways to the back fields, where boys were playing cricket. I only wished I could share in the conversation, but all was Hindko. A horse lay half devoured on the roadside. Natural death had made it untouchable by Muslims, so the dogs and vultures were feasting on it. The orchard was filled with sour orange and guava trees, from which we picked hard green guavas, laughing and swearing we would not get stomach aches.

It wasn't until that night that I was finally brought to Sayyed's wife, living with her children in her in-law's house. She and Malika and I spent some time together, but never in private, and as I did not know who was who, we never spoke his name or talked about Sayyed at all. I was able in surreptitious haste to pass onto her a letter from him. Thus began the communication between the two of them. Throughout the year, Daud and I were able to get her up to see Sayyed a few times, under the pretext of visiting Malika's family in Peshawar. And by the end of the year, by the time Sayyed's house was build, we moved his wife and daughters up to live with him.

We had to build the house first, however. The large compound was now divided into three households: Kamal Khan's, Sayyed's and the Afghan refugees'. During the building time the women of the Afghan house complained that they could not do pashto, and could not maintain their modesty with all these men working in their courtyard. They would sit inside together, quietly, bored, sighing, unable to enjoy the sun, the only natural source of heat in winter. I told them to be patient, that the wall dividing the properties would just take a few days. But the men were slow to work, and the Afghan women waited, squatted on the mud floor in their black veils, waiting as they had for three years now, for their country to be free, waiting to go home. They were living a life in transit, not investing more than for the simplest daily need. How long could or would the waiting last? One washed her hair, another braided it for her in the light of the open door, afraid to go out. They spent the days rocking the undersized babies, wrapped in rags and slung in rags tied to hang a hammock from the legs of the cot.

Back in Kamal Khan's house, I spent time with Ulicha and the other women. Here, there was no living with the men at all. They spent their time in the bazaar, or in the guest house. The older boys would come into the house only to get the flat baskets of food which they would carry out to the guest house, which was kept clean, carpeted, decorated and well heated in winter. The women remained in the house with the chickens, goats, cows and guns hung on the walls. The closest we saw to a carpet was a piece of cardboard, no cleaner than the floor itself, but on which we never wore shoes. We sat in spit, peels, chicken droppings, and baby pee all day. There were no low stools here to separate the women from the filth. And whenever a man did enter to get something or bring in dirty dishes, he always stood or sat on the cots. We prepared the food and sent it out to the men, eating only whatever they returned. When a chicken was killed, the men were sent the main pieces while we divided up the neck and carcass among ourselves and the children.

I was learning to accept all this and take it for granted, learning to ignore and turn my back to men or even leave discreetly when they entered the room, learning to ignore the filth and animals I lived with, learning not to mind being touched by ten women at once, to eat men's leftovers, learning to know men only by hearsay, their names, or by the empty dishes returned from the guest house that told me if they were good eaters.

I spent many weeks in this compound, returning on multiple occasions over the years. I felt like I knew the family relatively well, and felt very relaxed whenever visiting. One night Ulicha and I were laughing after dinner, and she was sewing me an Afridi dress. We had a gas lamp burning, as the electricity had been completely cut throughout the tribal area for the past month. Ulicha had just allowed me to tape the story of her wedding, and she and her daughters were laughing at listening to her voice replay when her eldest son entered. The tape was quickly turned off and put away, and we all choked down our laughter while he sullenly sat along in a dark corner of the room. There was no question of laughing or having fun in the presence of a man. There was no sharing of emotions between the two worlds.

As soon as the young man left, our amusements resumed. Ulicha wanted to sew the pocket at chest level because it was so deep and she didn't want it showing from under the dress. I tried explaining I'd look like a monkey scratching my armpit whenever I dug inside the pocket, and was demonstrating, which sent one of the women into a fit of laughter. She remained sitting there, mouth wide open exposing all her teeth, eyes squinted, allowing me only to guess they were fixed on me. I thought she was choking, as a baby who cries so hard he stops inhaling. Our laughing died to silence. "Jinn," they all explained at once to me. "The jinns have possessed her. She'll be alright." But she just kept on laughing, unawares, and after about four or five minutes, her mouth suddenly dropped, her head feel to one side and her eyes closed. We watched her in silence, and Ulicha caught her as she finally fell over. She lay unconscious on the floor for ten minutes, and when she did come to, she remembered nothing of the whole incident. Ulicha told me it happened once in a while when she had a good laugh.

Sayyed bought a minivan and began working a taxi service in the northern tribal area. One day in Spring, even though some tribals had come to Kamal Khan and warned him against hosting a foreigner, he and Sayyed wanted to take Ulicha and me to her natal village of Leshora in the Tirah for a wedding. Sayyed would pass me for his niece from Kohat, who wanted to learn about the Afridi area, and this would explain my non-Afridi accent.

Our trip began by trying to get gas in Jamrud bazaar. Of course, there was none, and Sayyed had to send a young man outside of tribal area in a pick-up to get a few gallons. Meanwhile, we parked in a quiet spot in Jamrud to wait. Ulicha and I were in our full burkas in the back seat, she harshly whispering for me to shut up every time a man passed by. Kamal Khan and Sayyed walked around the bazaar, bringing us back occasional cups of tea, peanuts, sugar cane, cotton candy, oranges, and more. They bought supplies to bring up to the village, where there is nothing. But the two of us had to remain stuffed up in the heat, stifled behind our burkas, the curtains and windows shut tight. Ulicha was ill, but the men could not bring us the fresh air we needed.

When we did finally take off, it was a beautiful drive following a dry riverbed all the way up the valley of barren mountains. People who live in these independent and remote areas live on the pride of their freedom. They don't allow anyone to meddle, and have an exaggerated fear and mistrust of any outsider. For them, explained Kamal Khan, all foreigners were Russian, and hence the worst enemy. So it was a test to see what a good Pashtun I could be. It was a test of my knowledge of Pashtun etiquette. I could not arouse suspicion, or there would be trouble for everyone involved. There was no question of going on foot in case anyone who knew me from before would recognize me and yell in warning. I was disappointed, as it was a beautiful expedition, made for pedestrians and not a minivan. I checked with Sayyed when Kamal was telling me about all the inherent dangers, but he seemed to wave it off, assuring me it would be alright.

In these mountains, houses were made of stone rather than mud, and they stood in clumps of three to four, always perched on high elevations with good views. It was still early when we reached Leshora. Ulicha and I left our burkas in the van and walked up the hill , following the path to the houses. I had to go straight to the main house, Kamal Khan's brother's house, while Ulicha went right and left to all the houses. I was not to circulate, but to sit like a tied cow and keep quiet, accepting the hospitality bestowed me. It seemed like an endless wait before a young woman came to take me for a walk. I suddenly felt how weak I had become over the months of not being allowed to move. This young woman was strong, surefooted and rapid as she made her way up rocky, slaty cliffs and back down again. I did my best to follow, feeling every muscle gone from my body, gripping my plastic slip-on sandals with my toes to keep them on. We stopped occasionally in the shade of a single tree to view the country and catch MY breath. We could see beyond Jamrud and on to the Peshawar Valley. My escort took me to the defense battlements, where the village men come to fire their guns from when there are hostilities with another village over an agricultural plot.

As we walked and talked, the young woman suddenly told me to be still. There was a man sitting below the boulders. But he had heard us, and as we stood staring quietly from a distance, he stood up and moved away. Apparently he had disappeared from the village some five or six months ago to go gamble, something utterly unacceptable here. Now, my friend explained, he couldn't come home for fear that his father shoot him, so he roamed the hills wild, eating what he could find. The fact that we had seen him caused a stir of gossip when we returned from our walk.

Ulicha went off for visits throughout the afternoon, leaving me in the main house where Sayyed also remained in the guest house, although I never saw him. As usual, we sent the men a beautiful wicker basket of food, and only ate when their leftovers were returned, though it was just as good. Up here where there are no utilities, the job of getting thorny firewood from the mountains is the women's. They also fetch water from a source below where, I was informed, the water is always warm in winter and cold in summer.

When Ulicha took off for the wedding, I was again left behind to watch the procession of black veils disappear over the mountain. Throughout the entire day and night was a constant firing of guns to mark the event. I sat in the house with Kamal's sister-in-law, watching the kids, preparing a potato stew for the night, and keeping the goats out of everything. We milked the goats and cow, and boiled the milk.

And then, after dinner, we, too, headed out for the wedding celebration.. The same young woman I had been walking with earlier wrapped her baby into a basket carried on her head, and another youngster under her arm. Thank goodness the moon was bright and we could clearly see every stone along the path, because I was still in plastic slip-ons. I was learning! When we entered the large mountainside cave, closed off with a stone wall and wooden door, only the youngest girls were in a circle, all garishly dressed, singing and banging on a two-gallon gas tank for a drum.

The woman were all seated in groups according to age and experience, of which there were four: the youngest girls, the young unmarried (aged eight to fifteen), the young mothers, and the old women, grandmothers now released from duties, who simply direct the household. I saw Ulicha seated in this last group, which I found the most interesting but could not join. In fact, I "belonged" to no particularly group. By the fact that I had no children and was not yet married in 1983, I was often lumped into the young adolescent group.

The night was filled with singing and some dancing in our sealed cave which, I believed, usually served as the goat stable. But as it was dark and spirits were high, no one paid much mind to what we were sitting on. Anyway, it was familiar ground to most women here. We had lain a large straw mat inside our cave, but it was filthy with babies' urine, spilled tea, sticky sweets and in the end with henna. A huge metal tray of henna had been brought in, which we all splattered and pasted over our hands an feet, spreading it all over as we sat smothered one on top of the other in our cave. As we all sat there with our hands up in the air to dry our henna, a vivacious woman began to sing songs in the Tirah format. The joking and laughing went on all night, and we all slept on the floor there flopped over each other, while the guns shot off incessantly outside. I wondered where the goats were sleeping that night.

After we had left Leshora, laden with firewood, chickens and walnuts as gifts, we returned with Sayyed to Kamal Khan's compound to be met with the news that someone had heard about a strong, healthy, young girl who lived up in the Khyber. Kamal Khan decided right at that moment to purchase her for his oldest nephew, but Sayyed and I, separately, argued that Ulicha and the boy's mother should maybe have a look at this perspective bride before engaging in any deals. Was she pretty? Did she speak well? Could she cook well? Did she have physical defects? All these issues seemed important to consider. I told Ulicha she wouldn't pay for a cow before seeing it, so why a woman? I was left feeling it really didn't matter, as long as the girl could cook bread and produce children. For the rest, a man here doesn't spend any time with his wife, so why should he care what she is like socially?

Ulicha wouldn't go, so it was decided I would go, escorted by Kamal Khan, to visit the girl and her family. He would discuss the business end of things with her father, while I would visit with the girl and check her out. I was able to report on her, and the families were joined soon thereafter.

I remained in contact with Sayyed even when away from Pakistan, and when I returned two years later, with my own baby daughter this time, and was settling into a rented house in Peshawar, he sent me his son with a gift, a wrought iron swing cradle. I continued to visit him and his family regularly when there, and kept corresponding when not. Today, I keep in touch through Sayyed's son's, one of whom is in London, the other in Canada.

13

Fortress in the Khyber

II. GHRA KALA (MOUNTAIN VILLAGE)

Qalandar Mohmand, a renowned literary poet I knew well from Peshawar, had sent me to his friend, Ayub Saber, a librarian and poet in Kohat, one of only few single men I have ever encountered in the NWFP. Saber was an overweight man in his forties wearing glasses and never really looking at anyone, only listening to his interlocutors briefly before continuing his own diatribes. I found this to be standard procedure for most discourse among Pashtuns, where status, be it social, tribal, political or other, is always present, even in patterns of discourse. On the contrary, the inferior speaker listens to the elder or superior speaker, and then asks them questions. The main difference with my engaging in discussions as an outsider was that, with certain people, albeit difficult, I fought to establish equal ground, with neither party deferring to the other. This was not always possible with everyone.

With Ayub Saber, however, I felt very comfortable, talking openly about a variety of topics, without feeling overwhelmed by formality or forced conversation. One morning I was following him through the ankle-deep mud of Pir Khel, his village outside Kohat, from where we took a rickshaw to the government bus station. Always puffing on a cigarette, this time he sent me to Mitta Khel, a village just beyond Karak in the heart of the Khattak area, and to yet another connection: Musamar Khan. Karak is the administrative center for the Barak Khattaks, one of the five branches of the Khattak tribe. They are spread out from Lachey to Karak, including Ahmadi Banda, the village I spent considerable time in.

15

Ahmadi Banda sits midway between Kohat and Karak, so the bus stopped there for lunch, where I recognized one of my friend's sons in the bazaar, though it was not appropriate for either of us to approach the other. The drive beyond this point was mostly through very jagged, desert mountains ranging from reds to greys, patched in white from the salt in them. Most of Pakistan's rock salt is extracted from this mountainous region. There was not a soul to be seen, and only a very occasional lone tree, donkey, or camel. Suddenly, we emerged from the mountains and into the sand plains, green and cultivated with wheat and mustard as far as I could see. I wondered if peanuts were grown in this soil, as they abound in the area around Ahmadi Banda.

I met two people on the bus, both of whom knew Mosamar Khan and who were able to direct me to his house when we climbed off the bus. I was issued into the house and greeted by a mass of women and an old man, Ghazi Abdul Jabbar, who addressed me in Farsi, English, Urdu and Pashto, almost all at once, and with tremendous excitement. He read Ayub Saber's letter of introduction, indicating that I wanted to study the Khattak dialect and way of life, and he immediately offered his services as my teacher. A highly energetic old man, thin, with a white beard and glasses, he brought out all his diplomas and degrees, dating from 1941 to 1967: Arabic, Persian, Pashto Honors, Urdu, Rifle Marksmanship, English. He had written a small commentary of the Koran in English, of which he offered me a copy. "There is nothing to equal my work in the world, and I'm giving it all to you," he announced.

Ghazi Abdul Jabbar was the educated man in the midst of a largely nonliterate rural population. He prized his own knowledge highly, and suddenly today found himself visited by a foreigner interested in his work. He was thrilled that someone should finally discover him and his life-long study. He was like a gem buried deep in stone rubble, and finally excavated. And now he wanted to be set in gold.

We sat, master and pupil, on a colored straw mat on the cement floor, he talking a mile a minute in Pashto, Persian, English and Urdu so that my head was swimming, although I somehow managed to keep up. Of course, when I tried to interrupt to add something, I'd be told to listen quietly, and to just stop him if there was something I didn't understand. Of course! Now that he had appointed himself my teacher, there could be no conversation. So I would keep silent, cover my mouth with my veil and say yes to everything. He filled my notebook with verses from Khoshal Khan, the great Khattak poet of the nineteenth century, and also some from Eqbal (Urdu poet), Rumi (Persian poet), some anonymous Pashtun folk verses, and even some of his own. When I was able to recite some of my own verses of Rumi and Khoshal Khan to him, he was greatly pleased to see that I, too, had studied the same languages. He elaborated on all the literary genres of Pashto and wrote the names of all the great writers, classic and contemporary. He even gave me a full lesson on geography, including latitudes and longitudes, at the end of which I had to excuse myself. No longer able to keep up with his rapid pace, I needed to rest my brain a bit. But it was not to be. My lesson with the old master was perhaps finished, but a new one started up right away.

A crowd of twenty women and children had been sitting quietly assembled watching our lesson, and when Abdul Jabbar left the room, they all closed in on me with the flood of questions typical of a first encounter. Most of them just sat crouched under their black veils staring at me, touching me, talking about me with veils drawn over their mouths and heads turned. As Ayub Saber had sent word of my arrival ahead of time, the announcement had spread fast, and three of the women had walked two miles in the night to come see the Angrez (foreigner).

The Ghazi's wife presided over the interrogations. She made me think of a New York City police woman, though she could never carry her role beyond her own small village of Mitta Khel. She was a large-breasted woman who wore the traditional Khattak dress, rarely smiled, and exercised great maternal authority over every man, woman and child, deferring in silence only to her husband, the Ghazi. Her expression never seemed to change, whether respectfully silent or lauding her own wealth and efforts. And in her palm or pinched between her thumb and forefinger was an ever-present store of snuff, which she used to such abundance that she always sounded like she had a cold. She sat quietly next to me on the cot, eyes downcast except when she was explaining to the assembly with great authority who I was and why I was there. With a stick in each hand, she beat and chased off the youngest girls when the crowd closed in on us too tightly. It was over an hour of solid crossfire before the Ghazi's wife ordered everyone out so that I could write and rest. Again, not for long.

This time it was The Ghazi's son who expected a conversation with me. He was a young student of journalism, full of political rhetoric, but it provided a welcome change, if somewhat odd. He would recite memorized phrases and speeches in English, not letting me interrupt him, but if I tried to respond in slow English, he'd ask me to repeat in Pashto. He could recite memorized lines, but could not understand a word, much less converse.

17

His mother managed to shoo him out, and I thought I could finally sleep for the night, but she decided it was her turn. She held my foot and became maternal with me, while sniffing her last snuff of the day, her head wrapped in a bandana for the night. Her last comment, as we both fell asleep on the cots side by side, was to ask if I didn't have fleas, and that she would check my head in the morning. In all these months I had not given much thought to the matter.

In the morning, it was a grand departure from Mitta Khel as we headed out on foot through the mountains. The Ghazi was sending me to Ghra Kala (Mountain Village). I knew only that it was in the mountains: I knew not where nor how far, and had only taken my bare essentials - notebooks, tape recorder, cassettes and batteries. I had learned not to travel with more than what I could fit into a small satchel, a knotted scarf. There are beds and quilts in every house, and everyone is always ready for guests, so there is no point to traveling with bedding. And if your stay exceeds a week (the usual time for wearing a single suit), there are usually extra suits to borrow while your own are washing and drying. Pashtuns mock foreigners who travel with the bedding and utensils on their back, and who won't touch anyone else's things. When the Ghazi had told me not to take my sleeping bag because there would be all the bedding needed, I had no answer. And it was true. In all the years I spent in the NWFP and Afghanistan I never needed it except two or three nights spent in hotels. Otherwise, I was always a guest. And since when does a guest use a sleeping bag?!

The January day was cloudy and cool, with moments of warmth. We crossed the dry river bed, where the houses of Mitta Khel came to an end, and began to climb. I was accompanied by Ghazi Abdul Jabbar's younger brother and his son, all wrapped in blankets, them with their local *pakol*s on their heads and rifles slung over their shoulders. As I walked quietly I remembered I was in the tribal area, a very isolated area, and suddenly felt very trusting of the world around me. Everyone had an unlicenced gun, and no one traveled without one, I was told.

The walk was easy, and the view panoramic. Across the mountains to the eastI could see Jetta Ismail Khan and Lachey, just a three hour walk, but a five-hour bus ride with a detour. To the west, I could see Hangu, Thall, and Parachinar, across the Bangesh Valley in the distance. And due north lay the mountains of Tirah. Everything seemed so close from on foot. The air felt good, and my escorts stopped for a tangerine and tomato break at midday.

18

After lunch, they decided to engage in some quail hunting along our walk. We met up with another man along the way, who invited us to his house for tea and biscuits, sitting on a cot in the sun. Two more men joined us, fully armed and turbaned. I asked if they were Afghans, or from Waziristan, as most Pakistanis do not opt to wear the turban, but no, they lived just over the next hill. We discussed rifles: weight, price, cartridge capacity and place of manufacture, but I finally rose and went inside to chat with the women, for the two men had arrived with an unveiled woman holding a child and a live chicken in her arms. She had greeted everyone openly, which made me feel a great joy and release after five months of utter reserve, of rarely seeing a man or feeling comfortable in their presence. Here in the mountains, men and women sat together, and the older women even participated in the conversation with the men. Four women had traveled from Mitta Khel to perform visits of enquiry about health and condolence, so we decided to continue the last leg of our journey to Ghra Kala together. I was impressed by their Khattak dress: heavy, pleated patchwork dresses, heavy silver necklaces, eight to ten rings all around their ears, blackened eyes, and huge baggy flowered trousers with tight ankles.

Ghra Kala was a farm composed of eight houses. The family owned a herd of cattle, goats, sheep, chickens, and a white camel. The mud structures were of poor appearance, with nothing in them but essential living ingredients: straw mats, cots, bedding, trunks for clothes, and utensils. They farmed wheat, mustard, and cauliflower. There was a well about one third of a mile away from the house, where the women went twice a day to fill their clay water pots and carry them back on their heads, sometimes stacked three high. Water was always kept warm for tea.

Was there no gentleness to this life? Let us say there was little time for affection or sensitivity. Laughter here was harsh and healthy, never soft. I was awoken after a cold night by a girl lifting the quilt from my head. I had learned that keeping my head under cover created more warmth. "Get up," she abruptly commanded. I rolled up and over for my shoes.

"Have you finished your prayers?" I asked.

"Not yet. I've done my ablutions."

There were two rooms to our house, and I had slept in one of them with three young unmarried girls, as always grouped not by age - I was older than most of them - but by marital status. Two of them had shared one cot, another with a child on a second, while I had gotten a cot to myself, a real luxury.

19

It was barely dusk: the full moon could still be seen shining high over the mountains. In the other room, the fire was already started, and the women and girls were occupied at prayers and ablutions, each independently. I sat by the fire quietly taking in the activities around me, attempting to understand the kinship relations of the household. Tea was slowly boiling. Sugar here was only consumed if brought in, so tea was prepared with *gora*, a dark ball of unrefined cane sugar. The young boys were crouched, eagerly waiting for tea, and eating bits of last night's leftover bread before heading out to school. After fifth grade, they would have to go to Mitta Khel and live with relatives if they intended to continue school.

Girls reading the Koran

They took off, yelling over the mountain peaks, and their voices remained audible for miles.

What was I in all this? The guest, self-appointed to learn by observing and participating in daily life, but relegated by culture to a role of sitting, drinking tea, and talking. Hospitality is of primary importance among Pashtuns, and my hosts appeared to fear the neighbors would talk and say they made their guest work. I was determined to fight the role, however, all the while respecting tradition and this fear, and quoted the Pashto proverb, "The first day a guest, the second day a guest, the third day a household member." It usually applies to a new bride, but I would use it for myself. I decided to spend my first day working chores with Gol Begum, the oldest daughter-in-law of the household, an emaciated, gaunt looking young woman.

Breakfast finished, the next task was going to the well to fill the clay water pots. Gol Begum, with her deep set, dark, almost haunting eyes, two other girls and myself set out, each with our water pot and cloth donut to steady the round-bottomed pot atop our heads. They had insisted I should not go, and I had equally insisted that I should. They giggled, but Gol Begum was patient with me, allowing me to do things, tolerating my ineptitude and showing me slowly how to accomplish my task. I had connected with her over tea, when we discovered a mutual enjoyment of plain black tea with no milk or *gora*.

The well was a distance away and down hill, which they all walked with straight backs and unmoving heads. I could feel even my empty pot shaking on my head, so I carried it on my hip instead. There was no wheel for leverage here, so Gol Begum lowered a metal bucket about twenty feet to water level and pulled it up, telling me to take it and pour a bit into each pot to rinse out and wash the bottoms. "Don't!" cried the other two. "You'll dirty your hands!" But Gol Begum told them to leave me alone, and I carried on. I did accept, however, to have her lift the full pot to my head when we were finished at the well. I didn't feel weak, having always thought of myself as physically strong, but I found it was more a question of balance and posture, and I felt that if I did not steady the pot with both hands, it would fall over. None of them, of course, ever lifted a hand. By the time we reached the house, I had dropped one hand, and felt very proud of myself.

The next thing was to make bread for lunch. The dough had been kneaded the night before, as always, and sat in a huge round clay bowl. I had a habit of always, no matter where I was staying, attempting to shape and cook at least one bread which, it was agreed, I would eat myself. Sooner or later, I would produce an edible one, but I have never excelled in any manner of cooking. I had made two breads the night before, which were lousy, but I was determined to improve. And I did. Gol Begum watched me, patiently guiding me as to when to turn it over from the other side. We were both squatted by the fire in the tiny, smoke-filled kitchen. She left me alone to work, and I felt honored by her confidence. Three things have to be juggled at once when making bread: turning over the one cooking so that it doesn't burn on one side, flattening out a new one in the flat flour basket, and making sure the fire doesn't die by continually adding thorny branches and balls of dry dung. There are two types of flour here: a fine one brought from the bazaar, which the older people claim they can't eat, and a heavier home-ground one only found in private houses. In winter, they are obliged to eat the store-bought flour, as the home-ground stock is depleted.

"Here, we can pee and crap in peace, where we like," explained Gol Begum. "Down in the village (Mitta Khel), there are people everywhere. Everyone is free here." Her words echoed most remote mountain dwellers I have met, in Swat, the Khyber area or here, who take great pride in the freedoms of being mountain as opposed to village people whose lives are governed by rules. All around me abounded freedom and independence, as each one did what he or she had to, without bothering anyone else with it. There was constant motion, the continued rhythm of work and prayer, without ever a complaint.

Several women ate their lunch early and headed out with the goat and cow herds into the mountains until evening, so we saw them off and then returned to work. The mother of the house, an old woman was hunched over sweeping the main room, and I finished her job, laughing that in my country old people didn't work but sat around telling stories. She smiled, but took off to clean the goat stable, and I followed. We swept and scraped them immaculately, with scarves over our noses against the stench. Then we scooped up the hay and fresh dung by hand, put it into deep flat baskets, and carried these on our heads to go dump them over a hill.

I was glad it was time to eat. And today, I was not relegated to the guest room to eat alone with my escort from Mitta Khel, who would remain as long as I did. Instead, I ate now with the mother, Gol Begum, and three other girls. Besides a large basket of fresh bread, we shared a small plate of curried stewed tomatoes, another of turnips, a bowl of fatty liquid, and a dish of honey. It was then I learned about Gol Begum, though not from her directly. She hid her face and smiled bashfully when her mother-in-law, laughing, informed me that she was three months pregnant. "That's why," Gol Begum began, "I drink plain black tea with no milk or sugar. That's why I stay home and do house chores rather than go out with the herds or to gather grass. Each day, two women from the farm went out with the animals, and three went out to cut and gather grass for the stable and for basket-making. I asked Gol Begum if a doctor came here to help with deliveries. "No, no. We do all that ourselves." She had lost one son, and still had one daughter.

Gol Begum and I had hardly finished the lunch dishes in the sun when a girl came rushing to inform us that the vessel vendor had arrived. He was squatting against the wall with his enormous cloth sack of tin vessels, including plates, cooking pots, spouted *lota*s for performing ablutions and for washing after a bowel movement. Nur Sanad Shah handed me a *lota* and asked my opinion. "Is it good? He wants eleven rupees."

"Eleven!" I cried. "It only costs eight in the Peshawar bazaar." I selected a good one for him, and they bought thirty rupees worth of vessels, sold by the weight rather than the piece. The vendor had come all the way from Bajawar in the Mohmand Agency, and I understood his accent well. It was a pleasant release. Upon hearing his origin, I cried out, "Of course, near Nawagey! That's the home of Momen Khan and Shiriney." They were the characters of a famous Pashtun romance I was well familiar with. "That's right," he replied. "It all happened right there. It's all true."

I took some time in the afternoon to remove myself quietly and write, while a handful of black goats grazed around me. I enjoyed the rapid rhythms of their hooves on the hard ground. Not far from me I could hear the voices of two old men, squatted in the sun against the mud wall, discussing the foreigner who participates in all the house work and travels with her own bedding. The breeze carried over the voices of boys and women yelling at their herds over the hills. Voices seemed to be carried from all over, yet before me lay hundreds of miles of stark sand-colored mountains, darkening into blue, purple, and black in the far distance. I used to think what a deserted land this all was. But all over, people were roaming, hunting, gathering fire kindling, cutting grass by hand. I could see our three grass gatherers coming home over the hills now with great heaps of grass rolled in cloths and balanced on their heads, smiling at me.

That night after dinner, we all gathered in the main room for green tea. But the women huddled together on one side, leaving me alone to answer the men's interrogations. One white-beard in turban with laughing blue eyes and a bellowing voice, was aggressively teasing me because I was not Muslim. The evening turned on religious argument, during which I felt frustrated and very inept as I had trouble following his fast yelling at me, upon which he then laughed at my inability to answer his questions.

After stale bread and *gora* the next morning, I took off with three young girls and "Old Woman" from the day before. Many women in rural areas do not ever use their given names, but some kinship or invented name, so by the time they are old, their names are forgotten, and they just become "Old Woman." I was amazed how, in these mountains, every word could carry what seemed like a mile. And the singing, especially. I had found the context in which women could and did sing freely among themselves. They all sang throughout the day, dialoguing verses back and forth in response to each other. The group cutting dry grass sang on one peak, while the other two, sitting miles away on another hilltop, sang in response. And while they did this, Old Woman sang her own mountain melody. They knew I wanted to tape them, which is forbidden, so they teased me, calling my name and singing to me from afar, and then stopping when I approached them. Their great fear, as most Pashtun women's, was that I might play the tape for others, especially for men, and thus bring shame on the family.

"We only sing in the remote valleys when no men are about at all to see us," explained Old Woman. If ever they saw us, they'd go home and tell everyone about us shameless women who sing in front of men. We're allowed to sing at weddings or other designated occasions, but otherwise we only sing in hiding." So the day passed, as the girls teased and tantalized me from their perched squatted positions on mountain peaks.

The herding wasn't difficult. We would sit on a hilltop overlooking the animals, and throw stones to direct and lead them. That way, the women remained free to work on making baskets all day, which they always brought along. Each basket takes approximately three days to complete, and the men sell them in the Mitta Khel and Kohat bazaars. At one point, Old Woman suddenly rose and ran down the hill after two stray donkeys, her red patched dress and black veils flying. In staying with her that day, I learned she was not so old, since her oldest son was a young man working in Pindi. That explained her strength and agility despite her gray hair and wrinkled leathered skin.

We were heading home with the cows and goats when Old Woman was hailed by another woman over the hills, and they shouted through the distance back and forth. Although with my bad eyes I could barely make out the person, I could clearly hear the conversation about me.

"Who's the stranger with you?"

"A foreigner. She's come from a far country to see our work, what we eat, and learn our language. It's her second week with us."

"But it's a man!"

I had not worn my heavy blanket in the heat that day, and was thus going bare-headed, so to her from afar, I appeared to be a man. Our entire group exploded in laughter.

"No, no. She's a woman, but she's taken off her veil."

"Why?" came the enquiring echo over the hills.

"She was hot. She says she can't move around in it."

"Isn't she ashamed?"

"No, it's her custom."

"Tell her to wait. I want to see her. "I'll bring her a glass of juice."

And so we waited there over forty minutes, letting the animals go their familiar route home, while the woman, with her daughter, ran across the hills with a plastic cup of cold sweet juice, which we all shared with pleasure. Then she and Old Woman sat down, both with eyes closed and one hand up to their ear in concentration, and sang several songs together in haunting harmonies which seemed to sail out over the hills. They allowed me to tape, and I was extremely pleased and thanked them profusely, vowing on the Holy Koran not to play the tape for another soul in Pakistan, or in any context that could dishonor them.

Back in Ghra Kala, upon recounting the event, everyone's first and immediate question was, "Did she bring you water or juice? Did she bring it in a glass or a metal bowl (usually used for drinking)?" I assured them all that she had gone out of her way to perform the utmost hospitality by running at full speed across the mountains with a glass of cool juice, and they were pleased. This was typical of the type of interrogations I was subjected to after any visit. I was always asked upon returning if I had been served tea, how sweet it was, if the cups were good china, and if there had been cookies served with it. And the news was the basis of far-reaching gossip. It was a way of judging others' humanity and behavior.

Throughout my entire stay at Ghra Kala I felt I had to struggle to be allowed to participate in any task, from rinsing out tea cups or fetching water from the well, to cleaning out the stable or sweeping the courtyard. I was still expected to sit back and do nothing. Little did I know that my participation at work would make the news all the way back to the university at Peshawar and follow me for years.

On the morning of laundry day, I was alone in the room writing when Gol Begum entered with her large, dark shy eyes, as if she trusted nothing and no one. Her small mouth, turned up at the corners, and her short cut hair on the forehead as though it had been shaved and grown back, made her look stylishly beautiful. She came in to ask if I would change my clothes because it was laundry day. "We're all women," she assured me. "You mustn't be embarrassed. I'll give you some cream to shave with," she stopped short, "unless you use something else." Laundry day was also bathing day, performed with barely a pint of water.

Gol Begum, as most Pashtun women, did not shave their legs or armpits, but their pubic area. I explained to her that we do not shave

25

there, necessarily, but that we keep clean by washing and showering. She accepted this, which was a nice change. Usually, when I tried to explain to women one of my own customs, I was met with astonished whispers of "God forbid!" as they touched their ears in a gesture purifying their ears from having heard such slander.

As we were alone, Gol Begum felt free to ask me for the same thing almost every woman I met in the NWFP had asked for: whiskey. Somewhere, at some point in time, a belief was spread as to the effects of whiskey for women. They believe that if they insert a whiskey-soaked cloth into the vagina, it will stop the postpartum blood flow. Whiskey is very sought after, and especially so from foreigners for whom, it is well known, the forbidden liquid has no taboo. Most rural Pashtun women do not wash for forty days following childbirth, and the excessive blood flow creates a considerable problem. Gol Begum informed me that the same treatment was also believed to enhance fertility.

After washing the clothes and laying them on the roof in the sun to dry, I set out on a new expedition, learning a new task. That day it was cutting and gathering grass for the stable and for basket weaving. It had to be done each day, but I would only have one chance to take part. I was with a young woman, an old woman, and a child. They showed me how to strap the rectangular cloth with one end around my neck and the other over my head, forming a loop on my back which was to be filled. I was given a wooden-handled sickle and told just to cut the greenest grass, but I was not told how to grasp the grass with my left hand. As it was, I worked backward, thumb down instead of up, thus badly tearing up my hand on the rough stems. My left hand was a bloody mess by the time I returned home, proudly balancing my sack of grass on my head. And while we adults had been cutting, the child had been making a broom with the long dry stems.

It wasn't until later that evening, left alone to cook the pot of turnips and keep the fire going under it with thorn branches and dung patties, that I realized how exhausted I was. I cried in the smoke of my fire, blowing to keep it alive. I sat squatting in that smoke over an hour, and when I emerged my knees were shaking and I just wanted to retire. This was the day that would be rumored so far so many years.

I spent three weeks with Ghani Khan's family during which, at one point, a letter arrived from the old Ghazi Abdul Jabbar in Mitta Khel, officially claiming me to be his adopted daughter and legal inheritor of one tenth of his property. I was touched by the formal document.

My lessons in Pashto here were extended far beyond the language. "Cover your head," I was commanded repeatedly throughout the day in harsh, hushed whispers. "It's a sin to go bare-headed. It's not doing pashto." I became more proficient at balancing the heavy shallow basket of cow and goat dung, after having swept out the stable, and steadying it with only one hand now on my head. I was more at ease with the thorny branches we used to fuel our fires, but the insistence to convert to Islam grew more persistent daily.

"If you're going to learn our language, you must learn our prayer," chimed the family harem surrounding me each night. As they were becoming more comfortable with me, I was learning some rude crude talk and insults. One night, after Old Woman had fingered through my hair checking for fleas and lice, Gol Begum began oiling my head with mustard oil despite my resistance. The dry climate here can cause damage to hair, and mustard oil is what Pashtun women use. "You're learning," I was told. "You'll soon be ready not only to become Pashtun but Muslim, and farmer."

The day of my departure, as I left all the women in the morning, they stood crying in their black veils and bright dresses against the brown mountains. With a heavy heart, I embraced them each in turn, and ran after my two escorts to return to Mitta Khel.

Bride

III. THE WEDDING

Akbar Khan was a retired general who had served under the British army until Partition with India, and then as a political agent in the Tribal Area of Pakistan's N.W.F.P. He now lived comfortably with his wife in an elite residential area of Peshawar, compensating for his retirement allowance by owning a small marble mine in the hills.

When I first arrived at Akbar Khan's house in late August, everyone was already beginning to murmur about his son, Homayyun's, wedding. Homayyun was the younger of two brothers, but the first to be married, which was not what the family would have wished, as it went against Pashtun tradition. The older brother, Aref, however, a doctor educated in England, had once confessed to me that he had refused to have his mother arrange his wedding. Homayyun, on the other hand, a working man in Jhelum, had preferred to bypass his brother and simply let it all be taken care of for him. The most he would have to do was show up on his wedding day, be social with the family, and go home with a new housewife to keep his domestic affairs in order. Later, I would hear the women tease Aref with comments such as, "He's gone and left you behind! Isn't that a shame, now?" It was in jest, naturally, but had the effect of a stinging reproval on the boy's mother who, traditionally, was held responsible for the order of her sons' marriages.

Suddenly, on August 27, I came home from the university to find Akbar Khan's older sister, Bibi, the eldest of the family, dancing heavily on her feet with swollen hands twirling delicately over her head in the sitting room, and puffing away on a cigarette from sagging, smiling lips. She was one of the only Pashtun women I ever witnessed smoking: it had been

29

medically recommended to her in order to aid with digestion and calm her nerves, and I knew I could always turn to her to borrow a cigarette. She had gone that morning, with Akbar Khan, his wife known to us as Baji, and his two daughters, Abida and Rabia, to ask for the bride's hand. It had been granted, and a wedding date had been fixed. Guests arrived throughout that entire day, offering boxes of sweetmeats and congratulating Baji on her good find. The first formal step in the long process of a wedding was thus accomplished.

"Yes," would sigh Baji to her guests, "it is such a difficult business, and such an important decision. Choosing from only our own or other families linked to us by previous marriages, we have to select a girl best suited to our son's social and educational background. Naturally, for Homayyun, I wanted a somewhat more traditional girl, educated, but brought up in the seclusion of family so as not to make her life difficult by imposing novelties unacceptable to her. If a girl has been raised with social freedom, we cannot expect her to be happy with a man who expects segregation and modesty from her. To break a woman from her segregation, on the other hand, is usually no problem. There are all sorts of intricate details to consider such as these, and it is a very delicate choice a mother has to make."

Later, from gossip with Aysha, Homayyun's first cousin on his father's side, she told me about the difficulty Baji had had finding a wife for her son. "She asked me and I refused," Aysha explained. "She asked four other girls and they all refused. You see, for us who are asked in marriage by a woman for her son, it is SHE we must consider as co-habitant more than the son. For us, the mother- and sisters-in-law are equally important, if not more so, to the husband. The bride has to embrace her husband's family before she does him." Three months later, Aysha officially announced her own engagement to another cousin.

About mid-September one day, Baji said she needed to go to the bazaar, and I offered to drive her, seeing as they had no chauffeur. "They all prefer to go to the Gulf and make ten times more money down there," complained Akbar Khan. "So there's no one left here, and the ones that do remain, well, we have to pay them dearly now. There was a time when they would just accept food and lodging, and be loyal to you for life. Now we have to pay all sorts of benefits and securities, and we can't trust them." So I became Baji's chauffeur when her need and my availability coincided.

This was the first time I had ever driven on the left side of the road, operated a left-handed stick, or attempted to follow Peshawar's traffic regulations. It was already getting dark, and I did not yet fully understand Baji's spoken Pashto. She wrapped herself in her ample white veil and sat in the back seat, leaving me alone with only a cap missing on my head to complete the role. The first stop was at a neighbor's house to pick up two other old ladies in their white veils. The three of them chattered away in strong, high-pitched voices while I struggled alone up front to stay on the left. I cannot tell how many times I hit the door when reaching for the gear shift with my right hand. I did not know where to go, and continually had to interrupt the ladies to ask directions. What kind of a chauffeur was I, anyway? I told myself just to keep calm, that I would find things out as they unfolded for themselves.

It turned out we were going to a major fabric boutique. I let the ladies enter alone, and went to check the post office for any mail. When I returned, it was to find the veiled ladies upstairs, seated on chairs, the fabric vendor on a platform before them, opening for exposure one beautiful silk after another, while the ladies fussed and turned up disgusted noses and did their best to appear indifferent to them all. Baji's tiny, dignified dark fingers would pick out one silk and look at the reverse side to inspect the gold thread embroidery. The other women would laughingly tease and mock the cloth vendor's goods. But the salesman did not despair for a moment; he pulled out every wedding suit fabric he had, knowing perfectly well that despite their fussing and scorning, they wouldn't leave empty handed. Baji became most verbose when it came time to discuss the price, something she loved to do.

One of Baji's favorite activities was going to the Old City, in Qessa Khwani Bazaar, and simply meandering from shop to shop enquiring about and arguing over the price of items. She knew every shop keeper in Peshawar's fashionable Sadr Market, what each one had, and what they charged. For myself, I knew I could count on Baji for accurate information on high and low prices before blindly making any purchase for the first time.

The bazaar presented a main source of social outing for most of Peshawar's women who, although observing sexual seclusion and modesty among men of their own social class, could indulge in flirtatious encounters with inferior shopkeepers. There were those women who went daily, particularly to the cloth market, the Kuchi Bazaar, and engaged in shop talk with these merchants, heads held high, ostensibly with great disgust and an air of authority.

Sure enough, Baji walked out that day with three packages of flower-printed gold-embroidered silks, all for her daughter-in-law's wedding wardrobe. The girl would be given a bulky collection of such clothes, one of which, selected by her mother-in-law, would be her actual wedding dress. The suits had to be tailored, and veils dyed to match. Baji was very excited that evening, and for the next week we would take the boxes out of their locked closet and open them up to display them to inquisitive guests.

The official engagement was just a small affair, so insignificant I was not even made aware of it until it had passed. Baji, Akbar Khan and his older sister, Bibi, simply went to the girl's house to present her with the ring. Nilufar, the future bride, appeared traditionally dressed, jeweled and veiled, eyes downcast the entire time, while pictures were taken. Her family had prepared a sumptuous luncheon, but the ceremony was confined to only a few close family members. The pictures of that engagement party were the only visual Homayyun could get of his future bride until the actual wedding day. When we handed the pictures of Nilufar to Homayyun for the first time, we all scrutinized his expression, waiting for him to turn back to any one picture for a second glimpse. Not once! Not a muscle of his face twitched. He said nothing, and never asked to see them again, dismissing, apparently, the matter as trivial, and preferring to discuss politics.

As for Nilufar, we would not be seeing her again until the actual wedding. From the moment of her engagement, a girl observes strict seclusion, especially as regards her future in-laws. A village girl engaged to a cousin from the same house might be sent to a maternal uncle or some family member at a distance, to pass the time in seclusion until her wedding. Naturally, not all engagements among the Pashtun elite are as simple as Homayyun's was. Aysha had organized an engagement party for herself at the Peshawar Club, with hired dancers and musicians, and over eight hundred guests.

All the wedding formality would leave Akbar Khan ruminating quietly. As winter advanced, he pushed breakfast back to 7:30, and still he would appear each morning with a wool ski cap on his bald head, and a Chitrali coat of beige matted wool, carrying his radio with the morning BBC report, and Moscow's inevitable interference. He would sit long moments alone or with me at the table afterward, brooding over the wedding, or telling me his worries about it. He really would have preferred to keep the whole affair as confined and quiet as possible, but the family would not hear of it, and in particular his sisters and the other women. A wedding is in reality a women's affair: a rare occasion for them to take out their best clothes and jewelry, to dance and sing, and to appear at a large function. They are not about to let that occasion go by unobserved. There would be no way out of the great wedding reception held by the groom's family on the third day. Apparently, the government had attempted to restrict the size of these receptions, but there were a million ways to get around it, such as sending invitations that read: "My son has just returned from Europe where he finished his degree. Please come to a party to welcome him back." And, naturally, everyone knew it really concerned a wedding.

With a heavy sigh, resting his cheek on his hand, Akbar Khan would tell me about the rivalry of gift exchange between the two families. "If someone gives a black-and-white TV, for instance, the other must outdo it with a color TV, and so on. The whole thing is just a big useless expense and headache. But what can you do? The women won't hear of not having it. It's all such a bother!"

A bother to the groom's father, however, was developing into major thrills among his women relatives. The competition he spoke about had indeed begun. About a week after the engagement, we gave a reciprocal luncheon at home for Nilufar's family, minus the future bride herself. Some thirty people came to lunch, both from our family and hers. It was an occasion for Homayyun and his future in-laws to meet. Baji asked me if I could prepare something original. "They served us such a fine meal; we must have something even better for them. You and Abida think of something." We decided to prepare egg salad sandwiches to change from the usual rice and lamb dishes. And in lieu of the heavy oily dessert, we carved out a melon and filled it with a fresh fruit salad. The modern ladies of Peshawar, lately very diet conscious, wary of their traditional greasy dishes and ever on the lookout for novelties, were delighted, and Baji was able to boast her luncheon. Gossip had it she had outdone the bride's engagement reception.

Baji was continuously receiving visits from everyone to congratulate her and bring boxes of sweetmeats made with rice, lentils, milk and sugar. I had thought, when I first arrived, that I had been fortunate to be hosted in a house with just a retired older couple. I had imagined it would be quiet and conducive to work. But no house in this country remains empty for long. And in this elite society, women have little to occupy them besides going to the bazaar or visiting each other. Our house, also, though actually lived in only by us three, was never empty. At least thirty people came through each day just for short visits. And Baji, a great dramatist at heart, took advantage of the attention to add to it. She suddenly fell ill with nervous tension, lived on Valium and other anti-depressants, even underwent shock treatment in hospital, and spent her days lying on a cot in the back sitting room with a constant stream of lady callers.

Baji colored her hair with henna so that just the top and sides showed red, while the long braid hanging down her back was still solid black. These days she kept a long white scarf tied around her head and hanging off to one side, over which she kept her light house veil draped around her head. Fashion among the younger generation demanded that they wear their house veil very narrow, not to cover the head, but as a decorative scarf hanging down their back.

For the benefit of each incoming visitor, Baji would begin by talking about Homayyun's wedding excitedly, and then, when asked how she was herself, would recline on her cot and start her story again, in a weak voice on the verge of tears, eliciting sympathy. Every woman was issued a detailed account of Baji's health; how weak she was, how low her blood pressure, how she couldn't sleep and hadn't any appetite. They left knowing the particulars of her diet and of all the drugs she consumed. Each visitor would sit on the cot with her a while and listen, clucking her tongue and shaking her head throughout the diatribe until she left. It became a repeated performance for all who came, almost, it seemed, enjoyed. Poor, poor Baji! Sometimes, if no one were around, I would lure her into reading a little poetry with me, which she also enjoyed, in a different way. Her normal voice and energy would resume momentarily, but it was miraculous if we could get through two lines before another visitor would appear and the show would begin again.

Nilufar's older sister, Goli, began having an increasingly important role as the wedding approached. She had married Baji's brother, and was therefore part of our immediate family also, and could mediate all the news and gossip between the two houses. She came daily, and announced in detail what Nilufar was doing and saying, what her latest feelings were. And reciprocally, she would go report to her sister all that was happening in our household. And although there was no frequentation between the families apart from Goli, we each followed the progressive moves and moods of the other. Goli was perfect for the role; always giggling and chattering with airs of a woman forgetting her class and age. She was usually eager to be friendly, to tease someone, or let them in with laughing eyes on a juicy piece of gossip, lowering her voice and looking around her to make sure no one was listening. The playfulness of her nature was further lightened by the glitter she applied to her face, and the thick eyeliner she painted on to lengthen the crease of her smile.

As the wedding drew closer, the invitations were printed; in English for the formal reception in Peshawar, and in Urdu for the second party held for family and the entire village at the General's ancestral home in Boghdada near Mardan. In all, about 1500 cards had been printed and would have to distributed personally to each guest. "They won't come if they just receive an invitation like that in the mail," explained Rabia, Homayyun's older sister. "We verbally have to invite each one in person, the card being just for formality's sake."

Akbar Khan would dress up and go out for long daily drives to the Afridi villages in the Khyber, to Mardan, to Sawabi, to every corner of Peshawar, and every place there were guests to invite. Family visitors would take their own cards when they came, and a batch more to distribute to other members. A man with no limit to his patience, Akbar Khan would heave his heavy tired body home, dressed always in well tailored three-piece suits, and would sigh: "I can't find so-and-so's house. Oh, it's such a big bother, all of this! Now they'll begin coming to complain that they haven't been invited. It's impossible to include everyone, and yet we must! It's SHE who'll be insulted afterwards," and he would motion with his head to indicate Baji. And indeed, as time progressed, Baji bagan to get more animated during the visits, launching into long plaintive diatribes about how such a woman had nastily rebuked her for not having invited her. Baji would often cry, followed by her own imprecations in a strong high-pitched voice. The wedding was preoccupying everyone.

I came home from some work in a village one day in November to find Baji sitting quietly on a cot in the sun-filled back sitting room, sewing borders onto brightly colored square cotton cloths. "These will serve to wrap the suits up in," she explained. No two pieces had the same border, and on each was embroidered a different flower or design in gold or silver.

Rabia was also there, as she was more frequently these days, with her children, altering a gold brocade dress which had once been her mother's. "The styles change, you know. No one wears their dress short anymore, or their trouser bottoms wide." Homayyun had already begun his forty-day wedding leave from work, and was sitting with us sullenly, though he preferred the chair. He never sat on the rope cots.

35

I noticed Baji coming through my room with greater frequency, at any time of the night or day. There was a closet there only she owned the key to, kept hidden, tied to her under garments. It served as a kind of store room, full of suitcases, trunks, and a heavy metal safe. Baji would come in to open and close the cases at least five times a day now, rummaging through everything. Winter was on us, and everyone spent most of the time in the southern sitting room, connected to my room by a glass wall. Even if I were at my desk in my room with the curtains drawn, I always felt connected to the activity in the sitting room. We had spread a large dark red Bokhara carpet on the marble floor, which gave the room an even warmer, more festive atmosphere. Eight rope cots had been lined up against the walls, each with a cotton mattress and colorfully embroidered bed spread over it, and large, firm round ballasts to lean against, to accommodate visitors.

Traditionally, a Pashtun wedding begins with a henna party held at the bride's house the evening before the wedding proper. But we were to have a private henna party for the women of the family prior to that. It had been postponed, however, to just the day I was expecting guests from a village, and would be occupied with them all day. Baji had put a mirror in my room , the kind I had often fantasized owning, with a coffee color geometric border design painted delicately over a black ebony frame which curved elegantly. The mirror itself was round, and rotated on its frame so that I could simply flip it over to its black side when I grew frustrated with seeing my own face. I liked the mirror, and feared I may become attached to it, like I felt Baji growing increasingly attached to me. I had become more like a daughter to her who, coming from a traditional background of communal family existence, suffered from depression over the fact that none of her children lived with her. I had been made aware of this from the start by the family, but it manifested itself the day of our henna party.

When I came home from a walk and a meal in the Old City with my visitors that day, Baji was lying on one of the cots in the sunny sitting room in agony, suffering with a migraine. She had already consumed an unaccountable number of tranquilizers, Valium, pain killers, and now, groaning in semi-consciousness, was demanding a morphine injection from Aref, who had come home for his brother's wedding.

There were none of the habitual women's visits that day; it was extraordinarily quiet in the house. I sat on my heels on the edge of the cot and massaged Baji's neck, the muscles of which were taught like wet ropes, but she only moaned and complained that I had no strength in my fingers. Aref finally gave her the injection to put her out, and she slowly sank back, moaning lightly, her frail little body curled up under two blankets with only her elegantly down-turned nose and a few red hairs visible from under her headband and winter shawl.

"You'll simply have to remain with her," instructed me Akbar Khan with a matter-of-fact smile. "There's no one else." Meaning that it was not his affair. He and his sons were going for a stroll at the club, and their Baji would simply become what she became. "We can't do anything for her," he smiled and shrugged calmly at me, leaving me the job of watching her. I felt like a lady-in-waiting of a court harem, a special companion enjoying that privileged proximity extended to maid servants and nannies, which even family never share. As she calmed down, but still suffered the pain, Baji suddenly reached out to seize my hand, kissed it, and held it tightly in her own, against her cheek, until her grip released. Knowing she was unconscious, I pulled my hand away gently, and remained propped up on the cot at her head, reading in the sun. Her gesture, that sudden manifestation of confidence, had both frightened and comforted me.

Around six o'clock that evening the guests began arriving for the henna party. The first were Homayyun's sisters, Abida and Rabia and their six children and maidservants. The alone sufficed to fill every corner of the house with screams and commotion. I could finally leave Baji's side and go change. I wore one of her old suits, unaltered to match the new fashion. It was a white satin dress with a few flowers embroidered in black and light blue silk. I had had a shear veil dyed to match the blue. But it was an old-fashioned trouser, with a three yard waist held up with a rope up, making me appear more enormous than I already felt. The current fashion required young ladies to have their trousers sewn tight from the hips to the waist, and fastened with a snap rather than a rope, so that it did not bunch up and they could wear a snug-fitting dress over it. The fashion was also to wear the dress at mid-calf length, whereas Baji's old dress barely reached my knees. I was completely out of fashion, and looked awfully gauche, something I didn't realize the importance of until later. I had thought it wouldn't matter, that we would just be family. I certainly had not considered the enormity of the affair. I found myself participating in what could best be described as a special mothers' day in a nursery school. We were over forty women and children, including the maidservants and the Afridi tribal cousins from the Khyber.

It was shortly after dark when we suddenly heard the sound of drums in the distance. The procession of women and girls had set out from Aysha's house, just a block away. One was beating a heavy two-ended drum, another a large flat drum, and a third a cymbal, while two girls twirled and danced gracefully, each holding with both hands, a tray of henna. These trays resembled birthday cakes, littered with dozens of candles flickering above their heads in the night. Despite the cold, we all remained outside, thinly draped in our best attire: high heeled gold and silver sandals, and sparkling suits and veils. The point is to sparkle a maximum at a henna party, because it is always a night affair, and a festive one.

Village Wedding procession

I found the *attan,* the Pashtun national dance, to be a question of an elementary simple step which I was fortunately able to pick up quickly although, I had to admit, without any of the grace characteristic of the dance. When they called me in to participate they stared, expecting, I suspected, for me to break into a modern Western style dance. Instead, I took a spot in the circle and fell into step with the other dancers, maybe adding slightly more movement and a stressed drop into the rhythm.

I found the girls at this event shy and inhibited. I had seen some very moving dancing by Pashtun girls at a lower class wedding in Quetta, where the girls had moved with far more agility and less self-consciousness. Here, each one scrutinized the other up and down, searching for the minutest defects and imperfections, while sucking in their own stomachs and never dismissing their physical appearance. In this world, as at home, women dress and perform to impress other women, their harshest judge. I was realizing the mistake I had made in dismissing due attention to my own dress.

When we went indoors, Rabia and Abida had brought out two suitcases, and set them on a large open sheet on the floor. In the cases were all the suits of clothing Baji had had made for the bride's wardrobe. I recognized some of the fabrics as being the ones I had gone with Baji to purchase three months earlier. Everything glittered with bright colors and ornate designs. There were printed saris from India, expensive silks, satins, velvets and fine chiffons. Each of the fifteen suits scintillated; each head veil was embroidered in gold or silver thread. These would be the bride's clothes for a life time of formal occasions, namely other weddings. Of course, that may not be the case for Nilufar, but for many less wealthy brides, this is a one time collection they receive. There were six pairs of high heeled gold or silver sandals, and four evening purses. There were fine trouser ropes with jeweled braided and tasseled ends, and a full cosmetics box. There was a case of jewelry: gold, precious and semi-precious stones, in each of which was reflected Baji's own refined feminine taste. Many of the bracelets, necklaces and head pendants had been from her own wedding jewel collection.

Baji, thank goodness, had given the fabrics to Nilufar in advance, so she could have the suits made up to her size and style. She had given Nilufar the money to purchase her own shoes, purses and cosmetics. Not every mother-in-law does this. Most make up the collection themselves for their daughter-in-law, and it is up to the new bride to adopt the taste passed on to her. It is one method of transmitting a tradition and maintaining an esthetic taste with little or no room for innovation.

Akbar Khan's younger sister, a voluminous and boisterous woman who would not be denied her role, held each suit up above her head, crying out: "Congratulations!" The women of the crowded assembly could then see the suits and respond each time with their own cries of admiration and praise to Baji for her good choice and taste, even if they personally found the clothes frankly appalling. This brought glowing flushes of pride to Baji's face as she lay on her cot, slightly revived, but still milking her position of the ailing aged matriarch with her harem of ladies-in-waiting tending to her plaints and whims.

Aysha did not approve of the display and, several days later, insisted on showing me the dress given to her by her mother-in-law for her engagement party. It was of solid gold brocade, one of the most intricately worked fabrics I had ever seen. "You see," she had to let me know, "in my family we'd rather give one single thing, and make it the best, rather than a lot of cheaper things." She was referring, of course, to the wedding clothes her aunt had made, and I had to brush aside the comment and keep attention focused on the dress. There existed an old rivalry between Aysha and Baji, and I had had to tell both that I did not want to be in the middle, and to keep their dissatisfactions with each other to themselves. Yes, I had been admitted as a member of this family, but had to fight off the gossip and secrets or else succumb, in the role of an outsider, to being drowned from all sides by the trivial complaints of women who cannot afford to voice these within the family.

The bride, as is customary and according to what had been convened by the parents, had sent from her side all the furniture needed to begin a new house. Besides the actual furniture had come five huge metal trunks stuffed with bedding: cotton mattresses and quilts, all forms of linens and tableware. It had been arranged in the back two rooms of the house which would serve as the newly weds' wedding suite.

All forty-six women at our henna party had to see and comment on the bed, the sofa set, tables and dresser. I thought of my own tastes for obscure and disorderly décor, and I knew they would not go far here. But the women ostensibly wanted all the details of the clothes and furniture, be it for no other reason than the week's gossip. Even the local tailor, who had never been near our house, knew the intricate details of all the gifts which, in a wedding, traditionally take on more importance than the bride herself. What matters with the bride is of later consequence, and therefore not worth enquiring about so soon; her beauty, the children she will bear, and the way she will manage her house.

Throughout our henna party, the five or six men attending ate together, keeping a low profile and segregated in the dining room on the opposite end of the house, as solemn as always. Akbar Khan, or his eldest son, Aref, would occasionally poke an inquisitive head in to check up on their harem's activities, although they ran the risk of being ridiculed by the fact they simply did not belong. In this society, men can perhaps indulge outwardly in being masters of their household, but they cannot claim control or even knowledge of the intrigues and connivances that take place in these closed female circles. In fact, they never dared to venture further than the door, or remain more than a minute, particularly Aref, who chanced vicious teasing about being left behind while his younger brother was being married first.

It proved to be an endless evening of girls' giggling and a chorus of female voices bouncing around loudly throughout the evening. It was a luscious scene, an operatic stage setting. The married women had taken out the riches from their own wedding chest inherited from their mother-in-law. All the family jewels were exhibited: diamonds, pearls, emeralds, rubies and gold. Expensive, well-tailored suits and veils, each colorfully adorned with gold and silver, glittered to a maximum.

I grew increasingly uneasy with the evening's performance, with the flirtatious game and charm, and with the fact that forty-six women were watching me dance when it came my turn, and that they were scrutinizing my short hair, unpainted nails, unpowdered face and old-fashioned suit, altogether lacking in glitter and style. I was intensely conscious that these feminine spectators would report my every curve and movement to the men and friends at home, that women are known only through the medium of other women's observations. I had listened to many gossip sessions and knew that although little enough is actually witnessed in person, everything is known by everyone, and one can discuss in minute detail someone they have only heard about in a third hand report. I also grew increasingly uneasy with the continual school girlish flirtation I associated with mixed gender groups, and not adult women among themselves. Women, it seemed, were at eternal play with each other, teasing, entertaining, flirting. Once in mixed company – actually it only took a single male presence – the behavior vanished instantly. Outside the bedroom, men were rarely a part of women's everyday existence.

The following evening, when everyone had been invited to dinner at an aunt's house, I stayed home alone. Not for long, though, before Aysha and her cousins arrived to decorate the newlyweds' bedroom with paper garlands and tinsel. At the last minute we would scatter a large sack of fresh jasmine petals for perfume. Although an easy enough task, it took the girls three hours to complete two decorations, while I remained in my room and translated two poems of Ghani Khan. They came to see me afterward, announcing that they would now dance for me. It was the first time I had been with two young ladies alone and not in the atmosphere of forced deference to the elders. They taught me a few more complex steps of the *attan* before we relaxed over tea.

I told them of the unease I had felt the previous evening, and Aysha began, for my benefit, talking about the restrictions, the sacred taboos existing between men and women in pashto. "We need a revolution before any of it will ever change. You know, when I went to America and had to deal with men, I was shy, reticent, wore no make-up, did nothing to provoke, hardly spoke a word in their company. If those same men came here tomorrow, I'd meet them according to our law, completely covered."

Even Aysha, who was among the most well-traveled, exposed, determined and wealthy young woman of the Pashtun elite did not deal with any male outside her family circle. Nor would she ever be seen roaming anywhere alone, but always with a circle of female cousins, or her maidservant. She had no sisters, and her mother had died two years ago, leaving her to head a household of men at a young age. She had arranged and organized her brother's wedding, and had made her fiancé promise to allow her three days a month to return home and see to her brothers' and father's needs.

That evening, with Aysha and her cousin, was the only occasion I had ever had to speak privately with them. I persisted in questioning their diffidence toward men. "It's rape we're afraid of," began Aysha. "If a man so much as lightly brushes against you here, it's as bad as rape, and if anyone should happen to see the touch, or notice you exchange a word or glance, well, your reputation is absolutely shot for life!"

Reputation! I mused recalling situations where men had deliberately bumped into me in public places or grabbed me as they rushed by, never looking at me, even. I asked Aysha if, with relationships the way she described them, women did not develop a certain contempt for men. "Of course!" her eyes gleamed. "Isn't it obvious?"

Where honor is the driving force of a society – as opposed, for instance, to economic gain – reputation and its preservation become the motivation behind every act, every thought. Fear of losing it determines the limits of happiness. Aysha explained, "We don't want to change; we are honestly satisfied with the way things are." She meant her group of educated elite women.

Aysha's words reminded me of statements made by some other Pashtun women, who claimed they even pity us Western women who, in our freedom, as they put it, have no one to protect us, and are alone to fend against life's more harmful misadventures. Throughout my years in the N.W.F.P., women often claimed they felt security in adhering to the social expectations laid out in the honor code and behavioral role allotted to them. The social group, or family, is all a woman has to identify with and define herself and the sense of belonging to that group far outweighs – and is certainly not worth exchanging against – her individual progressive transformation, which could result in expulsion from the group. All this implies that until the psychology of the entire culture witnesses a transformation on this issue, no one within it can expect or hope to change as an individual. "Anyway," concluded Aysha, "if we did want to initiate any change, we would only make ourselves miserable because the society as a whole is opposed to it, and we'd either live in frustration and failure, or have to exile ourselves." And the Pashtun culture I knew was a long, long way from undergoing the dramatic revolutions Aysha had in mind.

I felt in the spirit of the occasion now, perhaps because I had perfected my *attan* and could act my role in the festivities. But I mostly felt warmed by the insight I had gained, and by the friendship gone beyond formal politeness. It was mid-December, and I had Christmas on my mind, though I did not discuss it much in this environment. During the following days our house bustled with wedding preparations, drum playing, singing and family excitement which left me feeling nostalgic for Christmas at home and for my own kin. The sitting room adjacent to mine had become a twelve-hour-a-day nursery for women and children. They sat on the cots or the Turkoman and Bokhara carpets in perpetual festivity dexterously preparing wedding decorations, sewing and altering their own gold-embroidered veils and dresses, and just chattering gaily. The old watchman's wife had even come from her village to decorate a tree with paper streamers, which was erected on the rooftop. The entire house exterior was covered from head to foot with a Christmas light display. Multicolored canvas tents were erected, one on the back lawn for the women, and one in front for the men. I had bought a pink silk and was having a new suit made for the occasion.

The endless female agitation and excitement these last few days before the wedding were overwhelming. Women arrived by tens and twenties, flowing in and out at all hours creating an incessant flow of whispering, gossiping, and whining in high voices, at full speed and in rhythmic cadence, making me work my language skills to a maximum. They came to inspect the wedding suite, the furniture, jewelry, clothes and make-up. Baji had finished decorating the wrapping cloths and now a group of five or six younger women could sew the suits up inside them for presentation. East sari, each suit with its veil and shoes and purse, was neatly folded and sewn into its separate cloth, then packed into the suitcase which would be returned to the bride's house. And the henna basket trays were being prepared and decorated with streamers and ribbons. The homey warmth that glowed over us again overwhelmed me with a gripping nostalgia of Christmas Eve preparations, and wrapping presents by a fire. But as touching as it all was, the lack of any male presence left something amiss.

A Pashtun wedding is traditionally spread out over three days, on the first of which takes place the henna party. It happens differently in every house, but is essentially a women's affair. We had had a small private henna party at the groom's house, but were now ready for the official one at the bride's house. We had been invited for six-thirty PM, and at lunch that day Akbar Khan, increasingly irritated, had expressed his firm desire to have all the women assembled here and ready to leave at six o'clock. The entire female assemblage on the groom's side traditionally proceeds as a single entity, to the bride's house. In rural villages, as well as urban areas when the two houses are within walking distance of each other, an impressive procession of drums and singing makes its way on foot through the mud alleys, while the men remain indoors. Our procession drove off in a caravan of cars, and entered the bride's house singing in chorus, the younger ones dancing with the henna trays sparkling above their heads.

Under the tent, about three hundred women sat in chairs neatly aligned in four rows around the edges, looking like priceless dolls, bored. All seemed scantly dressed for the December weather, but none were about to crumple their delicate clothes with shawls or sweaters. We from the groom's side, to manifest our joy at receiving a new family member, were the only ones traditionally authorized to dance, and thank goodness, as it kept us warm. The bride's family and guests, to show their grief at losing their sister, could not dance. While we danced the group *attan*, the old aunts and grandmothers showered one-rupee notes on us, which served as remuneration for the two musicians, who would make over one thousand rupees for the two days of entertainment. I had the feeling throughout the evening, as I had so often experienced in this country, that I was waiting for something to happen, but it never did. It made me think of the explosively warm welcome we would extend to someone in greeting, with hugs and a million perfunctory questions, even if we had seen them just a few hours earlier, and then would settle into silence, broken only by stories of gossip or what might have happened on the way over.

Rabia resembled a precious doll, a sweet and fragile woman, maternal but young, playful yet mature. She wore her mother's gold brocade suit that I had seen her working on at our house, with a matching shawl thrown loosely over her frail shoulders, and a small gold purse hanging from her elbow as she danced with both hands raised, as if waving to someone on a departing ship, her movement just constrained sufficiently for her long black braid not to waver. Her purse contained only one item: a book of one hundred one-rupee notes to be showered out over the evening. This group was content to sit and chat, happy for the occasion to expose their best attire and eat a sumptuous meal. The dinner was indeed beautifully displayed, delicious, well organized for the amount of people, and excessive as usual. Generosity being an essential criteria among Pashtuns, people are so wary of being called miserly that they would rather prepare in over-abundance to be wasted, than be accused of being stingy. This is one reason why weddings can turn into ruinous exhibitions.

Nilufar herself did not appear and, as her sister, Goli, announced teasingly, "We'll see to it that no one sees her till tomorrow. It is customary for the bride to remain concealed at the henna party although, once again, the extent of her sequestration depends on the family. At another henna party I had attended in Quetta, the bride had sat quietly in the midst of our party, buried under her heavy veil, so that only her mother, sisters, or close relatives could lift it occasionally to peek at her sorrow-ridden face. A bride is usually made up and dressed for the actual wedding day, with her hands and feet painted with henna. She spends this last night weeping motionless and speechless in anticipation of her departure, while the party proceeds around her. The ideal bride on her wedding day keeps her eyes down, preferably moist with tears, her mouth pulled down at the corners, and her face lifelessly blanched. The closer she can resemble this picture, the more satisfaction the women respond with, shaking their head, clucking their tongue and sighing, "Beautiful! Truly beautiful!"

At one moment Nilufar did emerge into the tent, tented in her thick gold-red veil so that not a spot of her could be detected, and assisted by her entourage of women folk, for she could not see a thing, and was weighted down by her onerous new jewelry. Homayyun also entered, accompanied by his brother and male cousins, and was seated next to her. The tip end of her braid showed from under the veil, and Homayyun snipped it off, to safeguard for life. And they shared a sweetmeat, though all this was done without so much as a peep at each other. All four hundred women and children milled around them cheering and giggling so that I could not get close enough to see Homayyun's face. Fortunately, I was not claustrophobic or timid in tight female crowds. However, I left the crowd momentarily and retreated, shivering with cold, to a corner chair, grateful for a moment's peace. As always, I was not left alone long, and was soon whisked off again into the party. Had the bride become more jewel than human? Prior to the wedding, the only concern had been her gifts and clothes; now it was her concealed appearance and her tears. As to who she really was, we would find out after the wedding.

The second day is the actual wedding day, when a mass delegation from the groom's house goes to fetch the bride and bring her to her new home. Again the event, and the meal, would be provided by the bride's family. There were over eight hundred guests today, the men being also invited, but kept separate. Once again, our clan assembled at Baji's house and went as a single entity. Traditionally, and still today in rural areas, only the men go on this mission. I had once participated in such a procession in the mountains of Swat, as I came across the wedding party carrying their bride in a covered palanquin followed by her male in-laws jumping, dancing and running, holding above their heads the trunks and furniture she was bringing with her. I had heard and seen the procession approaching from a distance, and had been anxious for the bride inside the palanquin, imagining a young girl being jostled and rushed at full speed along the steep rocky paths. But as I joined them, compelled by an excited, vigorous father-in-law who, without stopping his march, had grabbed by wrist and hauled me all the way up hill to the house to partake in the wedding meal of rice and mutton, I had been relieved to discover that that bride could see nothing of her mountain excursion, her cage-like palanquin being covered by layers of fabrics being offered to the members of her new family.

By 11:00 AM there were over one hundred women and children in our Peshawar house and under our tent, all yelling orders to the maidservants, embracing each other, laughing, and reprimanding recalcitrant children. It was cold and gray, and again, everyone was underdressed, but it was more important to look splendid than to be warm, and graceful smiles gave no indication of suffering. The musicians had arrived and we had commenced our dancing party, which we then transposed in its entirety across town.

The groom, his father, brother and uncles emerged dressed in full long tailed turbans, looking aristocratic and dignified. Akbar Khan had chosen to wear a black three-piece suit and karakul hat. Three days earlier, when we had been discussing dress, he had declared, "I know the fashion is to wear a traditional Pashtun outfit, but I'm going to relish wearing a full suit." He assumed his stance, right foot slightly forward, hands folded in front, body tilted just noticeably sideward and back, the fixed triumphant

46

smile of so many proud fathers on just such an occasion. He maintained the pose without budging through the entire photography session.

Assuming an air both of importance and of not wanting to seem interested in the chattering crown, Akbar Khan rounded up his harem and, at exactly noon, we headed out in a caravan of about twenty chauffeured cars, with two covered pick-up trucks filled with maidservants and tribal relatives, and an open pick-up for the musicians and gunmen, each wrapped in his blanket, his kalichnikov pointed upward.

The firing of guns is an essential part of any Pashtun wedding. The more firing the better, never mind the unlucky victims of stray bullets. I had been to a wedding in the Tirah mountains once where I found myself shut away in a sealed cave with thirty women and three cows, singing, laughing, playing drums, dancing and smearing our hands and feet with henna while above our clamor could be heard, during two consecutive days, the constant firing of guns from the men's party outside.

Here in non-tribal Peshawar, however, we were met with obstacles, as the government authorities did not welcome such riotous behavior. Two days earlier there had been, in Landi Kotal, a town in the Khyber border area, a skirmish between the Shinwari and Afridi tribes. The police had entered the Khyber Agency, pursuing a car filled with outlaws. Officially, the police are not under any circumstances allowed to stray off the main road into the tribal area, but when the car headed off the road and into a mountain village, the police had followed. They were then assaulted by angry tribals who set their car on fire and shot the police officers. Outraged by the encroachment, the Afridis wanted to close the road off altogether, but the Shinwaris were opposed, and fighting had broken out, leaving a large number of dead and wounded, and a tense atmosphere in nearby Peshawar, where the police had prohibited the firing of guns at weddings. Our tribal relatives would hear of no such thing, and Homayyun himself had gone to Jamrud to purchase ammunition, and had to pay the police a two hundred rupee bribe to bring it and the guns out of the tribal area. After some preliminary shots in our back yard in the morning, the police had come and pleaded with us to stop, but they had no sooner turned their backs than it started up again. Traditions as important as this are not easy to interrupt.

From the moment we arrived, men and women were partitioned off and did not see each other again that day. We women entered the seated assembly of our kind as a group again, dancing, carrying trays of dates and sweetmeats this time. I was beginning to tire of this separating of genders, and longed for a male environment and conversation beyond the punctuality and finesse of the meal. As with all these occasions, I was amazed at the efficiency and ease with which they catered to four hundred women – not forgetting the equal number of men on the other side – so that everyone could eat a plateful at the same time. There were no lines, no masses crowding any one table, and nothing ever ran short. The ladies piled their plates high with sweet saffron rice, mutton rice, veal, chicken, kebabs, spinach, halva, and fruit. They picked at their meal with dainty fingers and left more than half on their plates, returning satisfied and prim as ever to the main tent.

I heard my name yelled out and saw Aysha and her cousin calling me to the verandah to get a good view of the bride and groom. We were a group of girls and children up there, chattering excitedly from behind the columns, waiting for the spectacle with that same sense of expectation which constantly frustrated me. A carpet had been spread on a rope cot outside. The bride was led out first, exactly like the preceding night, only this time her female in-laws had joined her mother to huddle around her and help her blindly shuffle, all the while holding a Koran over her head until she was seated next to Baji on the cot. Meanwhile, the groom had emerged by the same door, circled by his sisters and female cousins who danced and teased around him while his father, brother, uncles and male cousins followed solemnly behind. Pictures were taken, always in a stiff and serious pose as if it were taboo to smile, date pits were thrown, and a general dull and forced enthusiasm filled the air. Five kalashnikovs fired steadily a few minutes, drowning us and making my thoughts fly for a second across the border to the war in Afghanistan. They emit a loud, dry, clipped, echoing sound preferred for weddings to other popular rifles and shotguns.

Homayyun climbed onto a second cot, which was tossed in the air a few times while he clung on, not looking very amused the by the ritual, his turban tail bouncing despite the starch, and the female crown teasing him with squeals of laughter. But even as he proceeded over to take his place beside his mother and bride, who still did not look at the latter.

I could not witness the bride's tragic departure from her house because I had rushed back home with Abida to prepare things for her arrival there. Nilufar would hereafter be a part of our harem, with no question of returning to her own. Of course, among the urban elite, a woman can often go see her own parents, as long as it is not to complain about her marriage. But for many women, the wedding day tears are authentic, and the separation far more dramatic. They will not return without permission for specific occasions. It is up to a new bride to adapt, to endure her new mother-in-law and entire in-law entourage, and make the best of it.

By the time the wedding car arrived with Homayyun, Nilufar, Akbar Khan and his sister, we had laid down tufts of a freshly killed goat's wool like stepping stones leading from the garage to the back door where she would be entering. The goat had been killed just as the car drew up, and the house boy was standing by all smiles, the giant kitchen knife still tucked behind his back, to greet the bride. Her mission now would not be any less embarrassing or burdensome than it had already been. Seated on the sitting room sofa, Nilufar then became subject to a throng of women's curiosity. They were all family now, and were less inhibited. Everyone wanted to touch the bride, see and exclaim at her jewelry, pose next to her for a picture. The crowd of women and children was packed tight, hitting each other, yelling, giggling, cheering, while Nilfar had to sit quietly with eyes downcast. Her sister, Goli, had regained a crucial role. Being already a part of our harem by her marriage to Baji's brother, she was allowed here, and remained by her sister's side all day.

Baji sent me to get a glass of milk, which I stood stupidly holding, not knowing what for, until Homayyun entered, looking just as embarrassed as I, with the same frozen smile he had worn for the last three days, not so much as even side-glancing at his new wife, or manifesting anything but utter annoyance at this women's pageantry. The newlyweds, now seated side by side, were each handed a piece of cake which, without looking, they brought to each other's lips, assisted by all the girls standing by. In the same way, they then shared the glass of milk I had been holding.

"The mirror! Where's the mirror?" echoed a chorus of fretful voices. They meant the one in my room, so I ran to bring the circular, ebony-framed rotating mirror in which indirectly, and for the first time, they would see each other's reflection. I was moved, charmed, and suddenly lost to recalled images from Persian classical poetry, princes falling desperately in love from the mere portrait or reflection of a young lady. Nilufar's eyes went to the mirror, but Homayyn, flush with embarrassment, denied showing the slightest sign of curiosity. He was forced to peep, however, by the screeching girls who would have been disappointed not to have that pose for their pictures. Homayyun left as quickly as he was permitted, and his bride was led, still looking on the verge of tears, to the outside tent where we had begun serving tea to the guests. Giant vats of tea were boiling away, excess milk and sugar boiling with it, and we were to distribute cups of it, along with cake, to all two hundred women, including maidservants and their families, tribal village cousins, children, and our own family.

At five o'clock the older women lay down on prayer carpets and the house atmosphere was quieted. Nilufar, by then installed in her apartments, performed her prayers with her new sisters and cousins, who remained with her and kept her entertained till evening, waiting on her fully. Baji did not come near the room once.

Throughout that entire night, about thirty male relatives from the Khyber village stayed up in a back courtyard of the Peshawar Club cooking the next day's lunch for the reception, at which there would be over a thousand guests. Giant vats sat on large wood fires, and the men were quietly squatting in small circles, here cleaning rice, there slaughtering and feathering chickens in the semi obscurity. Akbar Khan had purchased everything of the very best quality, and in vast quantities. There would be the usual ground beef patties, chicken, veal, mutton rice, sweet saffron rice and halva. I had been brought, exceptionally, and after much pleading with Aref, to see the preparations, but my place in this family was inside the house and, more specifically, on the women's side of it.

The largest reception, known in Peshawar as the *walima*, is strictly a Peshawar affair, done by the elite. It is not an essential part of the religious tradition. In most cases, when the wedding party returns with their new bride, the dishes of mutton rice are served at that time, and everyone is fed on that same day.

Already the next morning Nilufar was at the breakfast table smiling but, after having her forehead kissed by her new "Mummy," she became ignored by all, especially by Baji who focused her energy on keeping her son engaged in local gossip, his attention diverted from his wife. Apart from the undertones of maternal jealousy, the new day embarked as matter-of-factly as ever, an anticlimax to the previous day's animation. And Homayyun, so long as he remained in his parents' house, would be compelled to puerile respect to his mother, and could show no overt attention to his wife. Nilufar was wearing a gold colored dress with pale flowers embroidered onto it and, of course, all the new jewelry. After all, these first days she was just an exhibition piece for people to admire – not to talk with, just to look at. Her new sisters, with me invited to join in, dressed, combed, and made her up, then escorted her to the Peshawar Club early to settle her on the couch and then went to welcome the guests.

Mrs. Jackson, an American diplomat's wife, was confused. It was her first time at a Pashtun wedding. She did not like the idea of being separated from her husband after they had been invited as a couple from Islamabad, and being told to go join a mass of women she did not know, all speaking a foreign tongue. She could not understand why the bride looked so dejected, so reticent and miserable alone on her couch, or what the purpose of this function was. She was experiencing the empty expectation I mentioned earlier, which constantly haunts the Westerner here, who wants a reason, a happening, and is frustrated by the lack of any. "Just to eat," I smiled. I had been assigned to look after her. "And it'll be a fine meal, because that's all people will have to talk about and judge the wedding by. The essence, the main criterion of the wedding itself will be its rice and meats. We'll just talk while waiting, and then go home afterward." I took her over to see the bride. "Is she pretty? Does she please you? Notice the gold sovereigns on her necklace." I found myself making the same comments and asking the same questions that everyone had asked me in the last two days.

The wedding formalities were finally over; Nilufar could now become a human being, and we could discover who she was. The first few days her sisters-in-law, Abida and Rabia, were always over to keep her company, as Baji would have nothing to do with this woman who had now come between her and her son. This was perfectly normal behavior, and no one seemed to take it too seriously. From my room, I would hear the three girls chat with distanced formality about the usual feminine topics – diets, recipes and childcare – each very versed in its latest advice suggested by Readers' Digest.

One afternoon several days later, I was sitting alone with Baji reading poetry when Goli came to visit. Baji's first words of greeting to her were, "Have you come to see my daughter-in-law or your sister?"

"Your daughter-in-law, of course, Goli responded pleasantly and respectfully, as she promptly sat down and took out some knitting, changing the subject and making no more mention of her sister, or attempting to go find her. I wondered if I should interfere, and go tell Nilufar her sister was there. Nilufar saved me the anxiety by entering herself, at which time there ensued some light-hearted teasing. The big topic was tonight's dinner at Aysha's house, and what everyone would wear, and especially what Nilufar would appear in, for she was still a bride on display. "I've come to do her hair," laughed Goli. "Who ever heard of a mother doing her daughter-in-law's hair?" Baji left the girls, and returned only when Homayyun did, not wanting to leave her son for a moment to "that woman."

I found I had the empty house to myself quite often in the days that followed, as the family was invited every day to relatives' for meals. One last banquet was thrown by us in the village home in Boghdada. It was a large open feed arranged for the villagers and servants, and the odd relatives who had not been to the Peshawar affair. Huge quantities of mutton rice and sweet saffron rice were ready early in the morning, and 10:00AM and 4:00PM continuously, about eight hundred guests arrived, in relays, simply to eat a plateful, take a look at the bride, and leave, satisfied that they had benefited from the wedding. Baji distributed some seventy suit fabrics to the women, each one according to her social status and how much money she had presented to the couple. Instead of presents, throughout the three days of the wedding, guests had offered envelopes with their names on it and money inside (most commonly one hundred rupees). All these went inside Baji's large purse and were later noted, in the short run to reciprocate with an adequate suit material, and in the long run to know how much to give each one when invited to their wedding.

The most hectic time was over. With quiet talks among ourselves we found Nilufar to be a highly cultured, well-spoken young lady, working on her Master's degree in linguistics. She had completed by first year in Peshawar, and would now prepare the second year privately in Jhelum, where she would now go live with her husband. She had lived in Morocco and Tunisia as a child, and spoke near-fluent French. She remained unequivocally subservient to Baji, attentive and respectful at every moment. Yes, she would make a good wife. We would be waiting for the first child now.

A few months later I returned to the house from some villages to find my room heaped with great baskets of sweetmeats, and guests inside congratulating Baji. Aref, perhaps pressured by society's blatant disapproval of his younger brother being the first wed, had perhaps also convinced that it was, after all, not such a bad prospect, had rescinded his decision to arrange his own marriage, and had let his mother take over the task. After a long a painful process of elimination, Baji had just that day found, and received the consent of a charming young girl in the neighborhood.

Women in Their Courtyard, Ahmadi Banda

IV. SETTING UP HOUSE IN A VILLAGE

Ahmadi Banda is a hamlet on the southern road between Kohat and Banu. There is no reason to stop there unless to visit someone. It has absolutely no tourism appeal, no bazaar save a few shops with just the scant bare necessities. Buses often stop in Ahmadi Bande to let passengers pray or enjoy a meal of tea and *kabab* in the roadside restaurant. I had been introduced to this village through Professor Perishan Khattak who taught at the Pashto Academy, and again through Aminollah Khan Khattak, a prominent lawyer in Kohat. The latter had first driven me here and introduced me to the Salar. If anyone non-local knows of Ahmadi Banda, it is on account of Salar Mohammad Aslam Khan, a former leader in the Red Shirt Movement, a movement led by Abdul Ghaffar Khan against the Brittish. He was eighty-three when I met him, living with his daughter, grand-daughter, and great grand-daughter. He was my introduction to the village and area.

The village had approximately 150 to 200 houses built up from seven original families, or clans, and a few newly settled groups, including mullahs, entertainers, and of course, Afghan refugees. The village was able to boast a boys' school to tenth grade and a girls' to seventh. It had government-provided electricity, with the usual vagaries of random brown and black outs. I remained a guest of the Salar two months at my first visit, and decided to see about establishing another long-term residence for myself three years later, this time with my daughter and nanny, while conducting research in the Khattak region. There are no hotels in the village, and no houses for rent as in the villages of Swat, where families free up their houses in order to rent them out during the summer months. When I had been to see the Salar about the possibility of setting up as an independent household with my daughter and live-in nanny, he suggested obtaining government permission to use the girls' school principal's house, since she resided in her husband's house in the village, and the school residence was vacant. It had taken some doing, but I did obtain the necessary permits, and arrived there ready to take up residence in October for the cooler winter months.

All the structures inside the village were made of mud, mud brick, and some stone. The alleys were not paved, so the winter rains made for constant mud. The school and its residence sat at some distance from the village center, north of the road separating the village in half, and across some empty fields. Adjoining my small house and courtyard were the schoolyard, and the watchman's house. A long discussion with the watchman resulted in that he would clear my house of all the school furniture it housed, and store it in a spare room of his own house. That would leave me with two usable rooms. There was no running water, but a public faucet which only produced water at a certain hour of the morning, so he offered to fill my water pots once a day in exchange for 400 rupees and meals. My nanny, Mina, urged me to accept his terms, claiming that if I didn't pay him, he wouldn't even allow us near the water. Clearly, she didn't have any intention of fetching it herself, and knew that the chore would fall on her, so she tried to convince me that he could, in effect, control all the water, and restrict us from using it. He lowered his price to 200 rupees plus meals. Mina then changed her song and pleaded with him that she would get it herself, that she knew my budget and that we couldn't pay him more than 100 rupees. He agreed, and we now had water for the residence.

That was the first item on the check list. The residence came with some cots and tables, so I only had to bring a small fridge, some carpets and some kerosene lamps and burners for cooking, heating and lighting. As always, I also brought Lawangina's swing-bed.

The watchman then asked about getting groceries for me, since it would be inappropriate for me to go into the bazaar, but I had already made arrangements with his wife, whom I became friends with almost immediately. They had a two-year-old daughter and two goats, and my one-year-old Lawangina enjoyed playing in their courtyard. I arranged to pay them 200 rupees a month for four services: her older children would run errands for me from the bazaar; her husband would bring me wood and dung patties for fuel whenever he bought it for himself (All our cooking was done over a fire in a corner of the courtyard, and since the region was desert, everyone burned dung); she would bring us two breads twice a day when she cooked her own (I provided the flour); and they were storing the school furniture.

The next concern was dairy products. There were only a handful of cows in the village, and few people had chickens. No one, therefore sold fresh milk or eggs. Most people used powdered milk. I was still nursing Lawangina, but wanted milk for her cereals. I arranged with one of the shopkeepers to send me a pint of packaged milk each day with his daughter when she came to school, and another friend with a cow sent me a cup of yogurt each day with her daughter in exchange for English lessons. Various people sent me gifts of eggs occasionally throughout my stay.

There was a distinct advantage to shopping without ever appearing in any shops. Many vendors cruise through the alleys of towns and villages yelling out their wares, and I learned how to shop the way other women do it. We would send a child out to act as a middle person between us and the vendor. The child would bring what we wanted inside the house, where we could scrutinize it and offer a price through the child. Vendors never saw me nor suspected they were dealing with a foreigner. I thus did most of my shopping from inside my or someone else's courtyard, and found it paid greatly as no vendor ever quoted me any price but the local one.

One big problem was the nightly electric brown-outs. I allotted my evenings after my daughter's bedtime for translating and reordering each day's notes, but when the lights went out and I was limited to a single small kerosene lantern, it doubled the efforts.

A far stretch from the concerns of moving into a house back home, but with time all my needs were met and we ran a cheery household, with a lot of little girls from the school to entertain Lawangina each day and to attend her first birthday party.

Young Afghan Refugee in Ahmadi Banda

V. DEATH AND LAMENTATION

It was in Ahamdi Banda when I lived in the school headmistress'house that I learned the news one day from my neighbor, Jansardara. Two brothers in the nearby village of Teri had died, stabbed to death by a common enemy. Apparently some tea had spilled accidentally on a worker in their house, and the worker had accused them of spilling it on him intentionally. He went home, and returned with a knife, to ring their doorbell. The younger brother, a tenth grade student, opened the door and was stabbed to death. His older brother went after the perpetrator, and was stabbed in his turn.

The teachers at the Ahmadi Banda school, with whom I was on good terms, had just learned the news and were talking of going for condolences since it was the family of one of their colleagues. They had arranged for a Datsun pick-up to get them at the close of school, and I asked if I could accompany them, to which no one saw any problem. Today, for the occasion, they had all worn their black fashionable *burqa*, as opposed to the white pleated one they wore inside the village.

The teachers here, all local residents, always did everything as a group. It was surprising to see them arrive in groups of twos and threes only in the morning, because for the rest, they remained as an inseparable group of nine. They spent most of their time at school, after showing the girls a lesson and leaving them alone to recite it for hours while they knitted sweaters and hats, and gossiped on the sun-filled verandah. It seemed a pleasant and respectable job. Another reason they were always together was that they were almost all from the same clan, the Dalamand Khel.

We all squeezed into the back of our Datsun, with our old school watchman to escort us. All nine teachers wore black shoes that clip-clopped harmoniously on the dried dirt and stone paths of Teri. We were an imposing group of ten or twelve, including two other teachers from the primary school in the lower village. Our leader, or elder, was Aftab, though her role as such was only played out twice during the event.

When we entered the courtyard, we were met with a slow continuous movement of women through the rooms and verandah, all filled with women crying and talking on cots. But it was still relatively calm. We removed our *burqas* and handed them over as we entered. I was at once struck by the old Indian wooden lattice walls closing in the verandah. Then we were received and embraced by three or four women who began wailing as they hugged us: "Oh, we've lost the boy! Oh, God! He was so young, so innocent...."

By the time we were all seated on the cots on the verandah, the teachers all had tears in their eyes, some more than others. The deceased's wife, tall, skinny, draped in a white veil, was led with sunken eyes, wailing and lamenting, to embrace each of us. We stood in line to hug her, each one sobbing with her in turn. When finished with us, she fainted on a cot. Another woman was led around the same way, but she broke down in a fit of wailing and beating herself, and had to be lifted onto the cot. It was then that Aftab, moved by it all, began screaming also, and we had to gold her back and calm her.

In all the times I have been to lamentations among Pashtuns, I have always been impressed by the tremendous show of solidarity in these moments of grief. Here I witnessed behavior not common elsewhere: general weeping together, leaning on and supporting each other physically, touching and holding each other, even taking each others' infants, a rare occurrence, for fear of being urinated on. These were among the most moving moments I experienced in this culture, perhaps due to the intense emotion displayed. Whenever one woman looked like the *jinns* (hysteria) were setting in, the others moved over to her, preparing to help her through the attack.

None of the teachers were personally related to the family, and it was from duty and loyalty to a colleague that they had come for condolences. So I wondered if it was not expected of Aftab, our eldest, to have her attack, representing the group's grief. At one point, the women on our cot were talking, so I took the liberty of asking for the story, and was given an abbreviated unofficial version from an aunt. Only later did I understand that it had been out of place for me to initiate the enquiry. There were precise rules of etiquette as to whose duty it was to ask, and when.

After sitting there a while, we were ushered into a separate room, where a tea had been laid up for us on the floor. We sat around, but no one touched the cakes and cookies, and the teachers proclaimed angrily that serving tea at a time like this was sinful. We each drank a single cup of tea, however. The boys' mother was ill with hysteria, and we had only seen her being led out of a room, past us on the verandah, earlier. The young wife was also too much out of control to do much talking. Now Aftab's role as our elder made itself clear. The time for the story had come, and when she saw the appropriate person, obviously a woman of the house, who was serving us tea and seeing to our needs, Aftab asked her what had happened. It was the boy=s aunt, and she sat up with Aftab and Najma, another teacher, and recounted the entire story with tears and cries. The boy's mother-in-law stood over me adding details to the aunt=s story, making it hard for me to follow.

Aftab once again asserted her authority over the group when, as we were leaving, we all had to wait in an alley for our male escort, who had stayed behind. We were standing scattered when some men approached us along the path, and Aftab commanded the group to stand all to one side and turn our heads to the wall. It was quick and subtle, and confirmed for me that Aftab was the group's leader, and not another woman I had earlier thought.

I attended many of these lamentations and visits of condolence and enquiry while in the area. I grew to understand them as a pivotal social event in women's lives, and they became the focus of my research.

Baking Bread at a Tanur

VI. YASMIN, A YOUNG TRIBAL WIFE

Dogul Khel is an Afridi hamlet in the tribal area near Landi Kotal, the last town in Pakistan on the Peshawar-Kabul road. It is in the dry mountains of the Khyber Pass where little grows and residents are left on their own without government or police interference. They pay for their freedom by foregoing the benefits provided by the government, like telephones, schools, hospitals and roads. The Federally Administered Tribal Areas of the NWFP represent land open to outlaws and refugees, who can come ask asylum and set up as house guests of anyone who accepts them. It was to visit Sayyed, an outlaw exiled in this hamlet, that I had come to the house of Haji Nawab Khan.

It was here that I met Yasmin, the Haji's younger of two wives, the prize and mistress of the entire female population of this walled fortress. The fortress, or village, is divided into eight separate houses, each with its own courtyard, animal shed, running water faucet, and electricity, three to five rooms, etc... They are owned by Haji Nawab's brothers and sons, all of them linked by a narrow mud lane that runs down the middle of the village. Sayyed was a guest here so, as his guest, I was now also a guest of his host, and was ushered inside to become, ultimately, Yasmin's guest.

Yasmin was the harem star and was mighty proud of that fact, enjoying all the privileges it implied. Haji Nawab's own large courtyard was divided by a wall, in order to give each wife equal space and a house of her own. The older wife, now less favored, had produced four daughters and one son, while Yasmin, strong, tough, proud and determined, had produced three sons and one daughter, and was five months pregnant when I met her. All the women and girls of the fortress respected Yasmin, consulted her and sought her advice in matters. She held the place of honor, and could always rely on a younger girl available to do anything for her. She was firm and domineering, but not tyrannical. Her voice was low, slightly husky, but not harsh. When she laughed, I felt it was earnest. If she was originally a local Afridi or Shinwari, her parents had raised and educated her in Peshawar, and unlike the other women of the fortress, she could speak, read and write a standard Pashto. It was an honor to be told by her that I spoke well, although I'd been feeling my linguistic skills digressing of late. I felt proud when, after visiting each separate house and each one's object of pride, whether it be the bread oven, television, or air conditioner, to refuse invitations of tea or food and answer that I was Yasmin's guest.

My hostess escorted me throughout the fortress, showing me the rooms filled with poppies, opium and heroin. In the corner of one room, a circle of young girls were working strings of black opium into intricate lace patterns that resembled jewelry. These would be sold in the Landi Kotal Bazaar. Opium arrives to this region in its rawest form in donkey caravans through thre tribal area from the mountains of Dir and Mohmand. And Landi Kotal's subterranean workshops and nearby homes, thanks to Germans who introduced the secrets of alchemy, specialists now weigh and mix. Squatting in the obscure corners, and produce pound upon pound of pure, unadulterated heroin, morphine, etc… And there begins the chain of connections that moves the drug finally to Europe and America at one hundred times the original price, and often mixed. Some travels by air or ship from Karachi, some over land through Afghanistan, Iran, and Turkey. The muleteers from Dir and Mohmand tribal districts receive the lowest end of the deal. In Landi Kotal the price begins its long ascent. That dealer sells it to his man in Jamrud, a town closer to Peshawar, who in turn transports it in fruit trucks through the uncontrolled tribal zone bordering Afghanistan down to Quetta, paying off huge bribes to tribals and then to police along the way. Bribes are paid up the entire line of officials in order to nourish this, one the country's most significant export items, besides labor to the Arab states.

Yasmin took great pride in showing me the house and wealth procured from this honorable profession. For each involved household, it represents an honorable trade, a legitimate, long-term and sound business, passed on from father to son, with a well-established assemblage of trusted connections. I distinctly felt like I was visiting someone whose back yard contained the headwaters of the Mississippi.

We would later eat together, in private in her room, and would lie together on her carpet that night. "Don't worry," she had assured me. "There will be no men with us. When a female guest comes, she comes in with the women, but when a male guest comes, every boy and man of the village stays with him in the male guest area to eat and to sleep. We will be alone here in my room, just you and me." This privacy seemed hard to believe at first, as about forty staring, whispering and sheepishly smiling women sat cross-legged in front of me, half of them holding a baby to their breast.

Yasmin went regularly to Peshawar. She informed me that her daughter resided with her sister there in order to attend an English speaking school. Yasmin also went to Sherpau clinic monthly for prenatal visits. My initial visit with her only lasted two days.

It was some months later that a message came to me in Peshawar that Landi Kotal had called, leaving no message. I could only assume it was my outlaw friend, Sayyed, so I had come to see, knowing he risked arrest if he left the tribal area. When I arrived, it seemed Haji Nawab was away in Lahore, my friend was away a few days in Jamrud, and no one knew anything about a call to me. It was cold and raining, too late to consider traveling home, so I remained for the night.

Yasmin's house had had a room added just recently for the winter. It was a small room, with concrete walls and floor, and a mud roof with two layers of straw, and wood joists supporting the mud ceiling. Anyone in the NWFP knows that concrete roofs create unbearable heat in the summer, and that mud creates far better insulation. But this was the first rain for the new roof, and it leaked badly in three or four spots all night. As usual, a large crowd of thirty to forty women and children sat cross-legged on the floor, packed into the tiny space, warm with its wood stove. On one burner sat a five gallon tin of water, and the other burner was used for all the cooking. The stove burns all day in this weather. A maund of wood cost forty rupees, and Yasmin could boast that she used one up in two days. I noticed that, despite the winter cold, everyone wore the same light cotton clothes and veils I'd seen them in during the summer. I saw no socks, no warm under clothes, no shoes other than the plastic sandals that are standard women's footwear.

Dinner preparations were quiet, during which the men sat together on the only cot, whispering flirtatiously among themselves. Each had a pocket mirror, and was smiling into it admiringly. Each had his perfume flask and hand gun, which he would pass around commenting, removing the bullets for inspection. They compared prices, weight, quality. Each was wrapped in his blanket.

The women remained quiet in the men's presence. I was served first, but refused to eat alone, so Yasmin, her three sons and some other girls came to join me. The men remained on their cot and would not eat with me. They huddled together, whispering and giggling among themselves, leafing through books of Pashto verses. They all ate after I had finished, and Yasmin ate again with them. Mistress of this entire village, she was confident and at ease with all her brothers-in-law. Even Haji's first wife deferred to her in everything.

When the meal was finished and we all were assembled together, no longer separated by our sexes, Yasmin and an agile younger cousin from next door, known for his impetuousness, his dancing, jokes, stories and good humor, began singing verses of popular poetry back and forth as is the method of singing them among Pashtuns. Not only was Yasmin's voice firm and warm, but she was extremely rapid to improvise verses to appropriately answer the ones sung to her. She by far outshone her smart nephew who, nonetheless, proved to be a good dancer. The evening progressed with much singing, story telling and laughter by all.

It was late morning and we had just finished a morning round of green tea. Yasmin, Haji's sister, a handful of other women and I were sitting together on the floor around the wood stove, when a nephew came in to take a pot of tea from us, saying there were guests in the male guest area. I appeared more curious than the others, asking him, "Who are they? How many are they?"

"How should I know?," he answered. "They're Kabulis." This was the term used to indicate Afghan refugees.

"Whom have they come to see?"

"Haji Nawab Saeb." And he took the tea tray out.

We would not be seeing them, we who all day would sit below inside this warm room by the stove. We would only know what the boys wanted us to know, and were capable of reporting. Ten minutes later, as we women were in heated gossip, the same nephew announced that a woman had arrived. He left, and two children showed the woman in. She wore a black veil under her yellow *burqa.*. A thinly sculpted face exposed a starved look, severe and far from smiling. Her black hair, at least the side strands that showed from under the veil, was neatly combed and held to the side by clips. We all greeted her, but the others turned their backs to her as she sat in a corner with her two small children, away from the stove. The atmosphere was cold, and I felt I must know more about this taciturn woman. She had just arrived from Afghanistan.

So, the border was not closed, as the local people seemed to want me to believe it was. The border would never close. It couldn't. Apparently, this woman and her family had received a letter from Haji Nawab, inviting them to come, claiming there was a place for them to settle. So they had come, crossing the passes in this weather at night.

"And where will you go now?" I asked the woman.

"God only knows." I was often met with the same answer.

Where exactly had they come from?

"God only knows."

"Were there many check posts along the way?"

"Yes."

Yasmin was being deliberately quiet, not even looking at the woman. I asked her if there wasn't any tea left.

"No," I was answered curtly.

Soon the nephew came and told the woman that they were leaving, and after she had gone the storm broke out among the women. Yasmin now yelled and cursed, and took a while to quiet down to her usual lively, laughing self. I didn't understand a word she said during her explosion, but later I was able to ask her about what had happened.

"I already have a guest, and Haji Saeb isn't here. I've got my own house and guest to feed. Haji Saeb has told a lot of Afghans to come. But when he leaves, he tells us all not to offer them hospitality. He's prepared some land for them further away. They must go there."

I interrupted naively, "But I thought that the Pashtun code required you to offer hospitality to whomever comes to your door?"

There was general uneasy laughter among the women assembled, and Yasmin looked around her peers for support. They nodded, laughing to each other: "She knows about pashto."

Yasmin became defensive, but persisted in the same affirmative tone and strong voice: "Yes, but not to everyone. If someone rich and prestigious comes, we'll go out of our way for him, but not for all these poor people who come begging. We can't keep giving them everything."

"But I thought that in Islam all men are brothers and are on equal standing."

More uneasy laughter. I had a feeling, from nods and teasing smiles, that the older women agreed with me, but they could not let down their sister. Yasmin continued, "So, now you see the truth, how it really is. We can't stick to the book. Look! That woman only sat here ten minutes. We're not under any obligation to her. Nawab doesn't want all the Afghans landing on him here."

I kept quiet, partly feeling it was not my place to challenge Yasmin's authority in front of the others, and partly realizing I could never hope to fight an entire harem of hard-headed fast and loudly speaking women. But the entire body of women who had come about that day were told the story, and it was repeated throughout the day, and probably to the men at night after I had left.

As for me, I had understood that there was a sub layer of rules governing the blanket hospitality that Pashtuns are so renowned for. These rules are complex, organized and defined by social hierarchy, prestige, and connections.

Mina

VII. FROM TWO LIVES TO ONE STORY:
MINA AND ME

This is an attempt to combine two stories. It is my story as a single mother conducting ethnographic fieldwork in rural northwestern Pakistan, and the story of Mina, the nanny who lived and traveled with me. Her story is translated and transcribed directly as it was told in tape recorded sessions over our five months together. It is presented in ethnopoetic format, allowing a visual presentation of her spoken word. My story of the two of us is reconstructed from field notes, journals and letters written at the time. The entire narrative combines self and other into a single text. It applies a self-reflective, qualitative approach to life stories, and is the result of a collaborative approach.

This story deals with Mina's and my constant negotiation of identity, with the villagers around us, as well as with each other. We were renting a house in Madyan, a village in the Swat Valley north of Peshawar, where the cool mountain air draws not only Pakistani vacationers for the season, but a growing number of Afghan refugees, wealthy enough to afford summer rentals for their family. My research, however, was limited to the constant, full-time community I had known since 1978.]

My mother's mother was a Hindu,
A Gujar.
Those are people who milk cows and sell the milk.

71

She lived alone in the forest
  In the mountains not far from Calcutta.
When she was pregnant with my mother,
  And there were three days left,
    Then everyone thought she would die.
She was all alone.
  Her husband was no longer around.
    Now, my mother was born.

My father's father was a Muslim.
  It was a very big family.
    I had twelve uncles.
My grandfather would hire women to work in the house.
  He would look at them
    And could tell right away if they were women of bad ways,
      And if they were, he would marry them right away
        So he could keep them without creating a scandal.
He had five wives that way.

One day my grandfather was in the mountains hunting.
  He used to go hunting daily to bring meat for the family.
Now, he happened by my grandmother's hut,
  And she called to him: "Son, are you a Muslim or Hindu?"
You know that Hindus can become Muslim
  But Muslims cannot become Hindu?
She said, "I've just had this daughter three days ago,
  And I'm alone and I'm ill and dying.
    Take her and raise her as a Muslim."
So he took the baby and wrapped it in his shawl,
  He threw it over his shoulder and rode straight home.
    He used to hunt on horseback.
When he reached home he told his wife
  "Mother, I've brought you a great hunt today.
    You won't eat meat today."
He gave her his shawl
  And she unwrapped it and asked, "Do I give it milk?"
He answered, "No, don't give it milk.
  We'll marry her to one of our sons."
You know that two people given milk from the same breast

72

Are considered brother and sister
  And cannot marry.
Now, they raised her on goat, cow and buffalo milk,
  And she grew up with the rest of them.

One day, when she was still very small,
  They asked her, "Zohra,"
    That was her name,
      "Whom will you marry?"
She grabbed my father's shirt bottom and said, "Fazl-e Elahi."
But she was just a child,
  So they waited a few more years
    And then asked again, "Zohra, you're grown up now.
      Whom do you want to marry?"
Again she answered, "Fazl-e Elahi."
  That was my father's name.
Now, the two got married.
A year or so later,
  When my father was out hunting one day,
    He saw a great ruby shining on the surface of the ground far away.
As he approached it, he heard a voice address him,
  "Fazl-e Elahi, don't take that ruby yet.
    Wait until you have at least one child.
      If you take it now your first child will die."
But he didn't heed the advice.
  He picked up the stone and put it in his pocket.
Well, some time later, his first child was born.
  It was a son, and he died.
Then eight sons followed.

Then, one day my father was out in the mountains
  And he happened to see a young woman carrying water,
    And fell desperately in love with her.
He had never eaten or slept apart from my mother,
  But now he grew sullen and kept distant from her,
    So that she finally understood he was in love.
Every night he would steal out and join this woman somewhere.
Finally, my mother could stand it no longer.
One night she cut her own forefinger

And rubbed salt into it
      So that the stinging would keep her from falling asleep.
That night she took the lantern
      And followed him out and saw for herself.
And the next day, she told him, "Fazl-e Elahi,
      You're in love with another woman.
          Why don't you marry her?
            Your father had five wives,
                And you are your father's son.
                Marry her."
He agreed.

Now, Zohra arranged the wedding,
      And she herself went from door to door inviting people.
          She wasn't angry.
            She loved her husband,
                and sacrificed herself for him.
My mother had then had her eighth son,
      who was just two months old.
After the wedding she left her husband,
      leaving all those sons, including the baby,
          to her husband and his new wife.
She fled, taking with her only the clothes she was wearing,
      and went to her brother-in-law's house, saying
          "I'm not going back to your brother for anything in the world.
          I've left him everything,
                and all those sons.
                He can want nothing from me.
                I'm not going back there."
Now, she remained in the brother-in-law's house for seven years,
      and never showed herself to her husband.
He never came into the house,
      and if ever he came near,
          she would flee into one of the rooms
                and keep her face covered.

Then one day, she was left alone in the house,
      as everyone had gone out.
Her husband found out she was alone,

74

and he was determined to go in and see her.
He made a hole in the roof
  and climbed down into her room.
    There he raped her,
      but as he fled he left his wallet,
        which she kept.

Three or four months later,
  she developed dark spots on her face
    and she threw up,
      like women do when they are pregnant.
Her brother-in-law noticed
  and remarked to his wife, "What's the matter with Zohra?
    She acts and looks like she's pregnant.
Now she told them the story:
  "When you were all out,
    my husband stole in through the roof and raped me,
      and now I'm three months pregnant.
        He left his wallet,
          and I still have it."
They all said it was alright and were happy.
  That's how I was born.

The day before my fortieth day
  my mother decided to go back to her husband.
She had accumulated a number of clothes
  and things at her brother-in-law's house,
    but she returned to her husband
      in the very suit she had left in seven years earlier,
        and told them to send the others after her.
She wrapped me up tight
  and walked back to my father's house.
    There, she was met with open arms,
      and I was immediately embraced by all of them.

My stepmother had meanwhile had three sons,
  and both she and my father were delighted,
    After all those boys,
      To have a girl.

That night, the three of them sat together in the room
  And talked late into the night.
When my father asked my mother
  if she would lie with him after all these years,
    she replied, "Not tonight.
    I'll lie with you for a lifetime,
      but just not tonight."
The next morning, my stepmother called to my mother to get up,
  but she said, "You get everything ready.
    Let me nurse my baby
      and sleep just a little more,
        and then we'll all eat together."

She got up,
  put on a clean white head veil,
    performed her prayers,
      and lay back down on the bed to feed me.
I was busy sucking when she gave up the ghost.
When my father came in the room and saw her,
  he teased her lovingly: "Come on, get up.
    Here you've been back only a day,
      and already you're sleeping in
        and refusing to give me breakfast."
But she was dead.

Well, they buried her in the mountain,
  and my father absolutely lost his mind over her.
All the love he had ever shown to my stepmother turned into hatred.
  He sent both her and her children away
    saying he never wanted to see them again.
  He sent me to be raised by my brother-in-law,
    who had no children,
  and he went and built himself a shack next to my mother's grave.
He spent one year there in isolation,
  mad with love for her,
    speaking to her in his sleep every night,
      until he was finally granted a place next to her.

Now that is a story of true love.
What do you want me to do with that husband of mine?
I spit on him.

Mina and I had lived and traveled together in Pakistan's North West Frontier Province five months before she told me this story. Afterward, I heard her tell it several times, exactly the same way, to people she met for the first time while with me. She never did allow me to tape it, but gave me permission to write it up. I did not take notes while listening, but wrote it up immediately afterward, based on my memory of the details together with my knowledge of her speech patterns and formulaic phrases.

Mina is originally from Bangladesh. She was married while still prepubescent to a Pashtun from near Mardan, in the Peshawar Valley of northwestern Pakistan. He took her home to his village, Gidar Gonbad, where she learned the ways of his house(language, dress, foods) and he treated her as a sister until she reached puberty, at which time the marriage was consummated.

I had just arrived in Peshawar with my infant daughter, Lawangina, for fifteen months of anthropological research in women's lives. I had been working in the area for scattered periods since 1978. Old friends there had helped me locate a small lodging to rent, but I needed an ayah, a nanny who would be free to live with me full time and travel to the villages where I would be most of the year. The person would also have to help out with housework like cooking, cleaning, fetching water, grocery shopping, and all the chores one can imagine where there is no running water, no electric power, no gas, no canned or frozen foods, or any other commodity we take so much for granted in the U.S. We would be living together in tight quarters, sharing meals and often sharing a bed when guests caused a shortage of bedding, or when we were guests in other houses.

In the space of two weeks I had interviewed over twenty applicants for the job. In most cases, however, the women were married with children and were not free to travel outside the city. Or else they spoke only Urdu, which neither I nor any of my informants spoke, and this would mean social isolation in Pashtun villages.

I had been in my new house only three days. Two children of a poet friend, Qalandar Mohmand, had come to spend the night with me, and the next morning I was rushing to get my three-month old Lawangina ready and the children fed so we could get to the university in time to meet their father. I had no food yet in the house, and sent the children out to get bread.

77

While they were gone, a knock came and it was a short, middle aged, woman with round cheeks who spoke a very broken Pashto. She started right away to tell me how much she liked working for foreigners, and that she was desperate for work. She began crying, telling me her husband had taken another woman and had chased her away, that she had no children, but was alone and could go everywhere with me, that she would cook anything I wanted, would wash clothes, would care for the baby, that I was her daughter and she was my mother.

I was running late and wondering how we would get to our appointment on time. I listened to her, but told her I had already hired someone, and couldn't just tell her to go away. The truth is that a younger woman had come the day before. I had found her nervous with my daughter, rattling things loudly to distract her rather than just letting her be and calm down. The other disadvantage was that she had a family and could only work days and could not travel.

"Chase her away and keep me!" said Mina. I admired her audacity at once. When the younger nanny showed up at the gate, she had two very dirty and sickly looking children with her, and I was suddenly very glad not to have to leave Lawangina with her. I told her I had found someone else who could live full time with me.

There was no time to hesitate, as I was so late. I left Lawangina with Mina, and hurriedly took the two children to the university. When I returned two hours later, Mina had washed all the diapers and clothes, and had thoroughly scrubbed down the kitchen and bathroom. The baby was lying quietly in her swing-bed in the courtyard, and a hot lunch was ready. That convinced me. I gave Mina the afternoon off, and money to buy clothes and bedding for herself. When she returned that evening, she had her new bedding rolled up on her head and a beaming smile and greeting. She walked past me straight into the empty room.

The following narrative is the first full life story I ever heard Mina tell. It was narrated after she had been living and traveling with me as my daughter's ayah for just under a month. We were living in the Khattak village of Ahmadi Banda as guests of Salar Muhammad Aslam Khattak, who had been an influential political leader in the beginning of the century in the country's effort to rid itself of British dominance. His household remained the most respected and influential house in the village. Mina was unhappy here, and quarreled with the women. I had known the village since 1982 when I was first introduced as a guest, but Mina was a newcomer to Ahmadi Banda, and her story was often asked of her, whereas mine was already known and merely needed updating since the last three years. The following life story was told to a group of five women and several children upon the women's request. I had been asking Mina for some time, and she chose to narrate it in this setting. From her first words, Mina had tears in her eyes, as did two of her listeners.

I am a very friendless person.
  I am very friendless.
    I am very helpless.
      Apart from God
        I have absolutely no one.
I had a very dear loving husband.

  But that husband,
    now, he took a wife for the sake of children.
  Saying, "I married the women
    to have children."
But she was a cripple.
There wasn't an ounce of humanity in the woman,
  or in the man.
And I got to it.
  People sacrifice cows and oxen,
    and I sacrificed my own self.

And I was ten years old when I got married to my husband.
  And I left my own village and homeland,
    and I came with my husband to Pakistan.
I lost my mother when I was forty days old.
  I lost my father when I was one year old.
    I'm very much an orphan.
      I'm very poor.
      I'm friendless.
        I have eleven brothers.
Then, I even came to Pakistan.
  I was very happy with my husband.
  I spent wonderful days.
When I got him married,
  then that cripple performed spells and black magic.
    She turned that husband against me.

79

I spent a full six years.
  I thought to myself, "We are Pashtuns,
    And I have no one.
      And my husband has paternal cousins.
        He has friends and relatives.
          He has a *hujra* and a mosque.
  And there's no one to speak badly of my husband.
    No one insults my brother-in-law."
With these thoughts,
  I ruined my own life those six years,
    Seven years.

Anyway, then my patience ended.
  I went to Khaki Chairman (local official) of Gonbad, near Mardan.
He (my husband) didn't agree to give me my allowance.
  I wanted the allowance due to me as a co-wife.
    He wouldn't give it to me.
      So I went to the landlord.
Then, there is a *khan* in our village, Salahoddin Khan.
  I went to him.
    He didn't give me my allowance either.
    He told me, "Take *gora* from *gora*.
      Take tea from the tea.
        Take sugar from the sugar.
          And cook it,
              Cool it
              And eat it."*
Now, these days mother and daughter don't even get along.
  How can you expect co-wives to ever get along?
When I asked for independence,
  The *khan* didn't give it to me.
    He made things difficult for me.
      He made things difficult for my husband.

With that lot on me,
  I took the road for Peshawar.
When I took the road for Peshawar,

80

Then on foot,
  I came on foot from Gidar to Ghare, near Mardan.
Then in Ghare, I got into a bus.
  Then I got off in Kalpana,
    And from Kalpana, I made my way on foot to the main bus depot.

Anyway, then, I sat in a bus to Peshawar.
  I didn't know the road.
    I didn't know the world.
And then, in Peshawar,
  I sat under a tree in Spin Jumat. (A busy shopping and hospital area
near University Town, an affluent residential neighborhood of Peshawar.)
Then God made me reach there that day at 12 o'clock.

Then a lady,
  She saw me.
    from her car.
      And that lady came back in her car
        And she told me,
          "What are you doing, sitting here?"
Now, I told her, "I've come looking for work."
  She said, "You have TB."
    I said, "You'll get me treated."
She opened the car door.
  The poor thing sat me down.
    She took me to her house.

When she took me to her house,
  She asked me, "What's your name?"
    I told her, "My name is Mina."
  She asked, "What work can you do?"
    Now, I told her, "I'll wash the laundry.
      I'll wash the dishes."
  She said, "How much salary do you require?"
Now, I thought to myself
  That she might give me 20 or 50 rupees salary.
    She told me, "I'll give you 200 rupees salary."
      I said, "Very well."

Then she asked me, "What village are you from?"
　Now, I told her, "From Gidar Gonbad, near Mardan."
　　Then she said, "Do you have any relatives?"
Now, I began crying a lot, then.
　And I turned my face away and thought,
　　"Now, what can I say to this Bibi?"
Now then, I told her, "Bibi, I have no one."
She drew me close to her.
　She kissed me.
　　She gave me a room.

In the morning when I got up,
　I did my prayers,
　　Four times.
　　　And I took the broom.
　　　　I swept the gardens,
　　　　　I swept the gates.
She said to me, "Has the sweeper come?"
　I said, "No, Bibi, he hasn't come.
　　I did the sweeping."
She said, "Don't you sweep.
　The sweeper will come."
Now, then, two days later, I started doing the cooking.
　She raised my salary to 400 rupees.

But for two entire years my heart was unhappy in Peshawar.
　I thought of my friends and relatives.
　　I thought of my friends and enemies.
　　　I thought of my husband.
And I'd built my own house,
　Mud brick by mud brick.
　　Mud brick by mud brick I'd built a three-room house.
　　　My mother-in-law gave me the land.
And I made a low profit where and how I could.
　I mixed water with milk,
　　I under measured weights,
　　　I cut four pounds into two,
　　　　I brought tiny chicks and sold them as fat chickens.
　　　　　All this I sold.

And I did it all for my husband.
I had a great deal of love and affection for my husband.
  I lost all my hair transporting sand in metal trays on my head.
  I stole dry earth clumps from the plowed fields at night.
    I kept my house clean.
Now, that cripple has come into that house.
  Now, not even a dog will piss in that house.
    When our friends and relatives come,
      They are met with the stench of crap.
        No one will even drink water at our house.

Two years later I was all set.
Then I came and went to my husband.
  She had so ruined my husband
    That he no longer recognized his own wife,
      Friend, enemy or sister.
Anyway, God has given me companionship and patience.
  God has given me everything.
    Everything I've earned in Peshawar.
      Everything of quality:
        An iron,
          TV,
            And tape recorder.
  God has given me everything.
    God didn't cheat me in anything.

And for five years, I worked for an Angrez Bibi.
  And now I've been working for Bena Bibi,
    An American Bibi, for 2 or 3 weeks.
She is very dear and kind to me.
  She tells me, "You are not my employee.
    You are my mother.
      And you will stay with me a year."
Now, then, I will work for you.
  I will work for the Angrez.
That's how I spend my time.
And what more should I tape for you?
  I will fill so many tapes with many many stories.
And many very great hardships have passed.

And now, I've earned so much in Peshawar,
  I can hopefully build myself a 3 to 4 room house.
And, anyway, God has done the rest.
  God Almighty has slowly done the rest with my own labor.

[BG: Has there been no joy in your life?]
  M: There is none, Bibi.
    None.
      I was only happy in life until I married my husband.
        When I married my husband,
          Then I became a door-to-door beggar.
        "Someone of good character needs only a warning,
          but one of bad character needs a beating."
            Try to understand what I'm saying.

And anyway, I've become fully disposed to this foreign *bibi*.
Now I've taped my own voice.
  Now, I'm a Pashtun woman.
    I've never taped my voice.
That's enough, Bibi.

[BG: Tell me about your co-wife.]
  M: My co-wife is a cripple.
And my husband had another wife.
  He divorced her.
    And he told me, "You take a divorce, too."
But I won't take a divorce.
  My name is Mina.
    My name is not a divorcee name.
      And my husband has a habit of divorcing.
        I don't accept divorced status.

Now, I've earned money in Peshawar.
  And I've bought some land for myself.
    Half an acre.
      I bought it at 700 rupees a section.
        And now I've built myself a house.
          And the deed is in my name.
Now all my earnings have disappeared with my husband.

Now, my last word is this:
   That I will wait a bit in court.
Now, that deed, I'll present it in court.
   I'll tell them, "Give me what's in my name,
      And give my husband what's in his name."
Either I'll win, or I'll lose.

   If I win, I'll sprinkle a little pepper on their heads.
   If I lose,
      Well, anyway, I'll keep going door-to-door as a wretched vagrant.
   When I die, dog pups will eat me,
         Or someone will throw me into the sea.
            Or else I'll lie in someone's shadow.
That's my last solution.

   Throughout the telling of this story, Mina remained very conscious of the tape recorder. She spoke slowly, loudly, and right into the microphone. We were in someone's house where the women had been exchanging life stories and tears over tea. Mina's purpose in this telling was both to impress these women of her worthiness as a Pashtun, and to assure that it was being recorded. She was both performing and fulfilling an ethical duty in self presentation. While the tape recorder was on, she and two of the women were in tears, while another woman I knew well and I exchanged smiles and commentary. The audience all agreed that she had a very beautiful story, and when I asked what that meant, they replied, "There's so much pain and suffering in it."
   When the tape recorder was turned off, however, Mina began telling her listeners about all the possessions she had accumulated over the years, and kept stored in her house: tape recorders, fans, furniture, etc. Two of the women laughed and exclaimed, "You have all that! So, now why do you cry?"
   These women, whom I had known a long time already, since I had first done fieldwork in that village, later told me they thought Mina was cunning, dishonest and manipulative. They, and many other friends and informants, strongly advised me to fire her. But I ignored them and continued to employ Mina, believing that she was irreplaceable. She was strong and unafraid. She was wonderful with the baby. I knew I could leave on short expeditions and trust her to run the house with the necessary

confidence and skills. I had trained her to look after Lawangina's water, feedings, diapers, sleep schedule and other details exactly as I did them, which was completely anomalous to local childrearing practices. And being an older woman of independent mind and character, she could handle male guests without fear or embarrassment. As I was a foreigner, I could and did receive, particularly in our city house, male visitors for meals or conferences. Mina always cooked good meals, conversed with guests and was not overwhelmed with the lack of gender segregation in my house.

Mina had a childlike mischievous side to her. Her face could explode radiantly with a little girl's excitement, and could darken as quickly into threatening rage. Her great passion was movies. Indian movies are filled with dancing and music, and these, with their stories, occupied much of her time.

Roasting peanuts, Ahmadi Banda

I often came home to hear the rapid, choppy movie song playing on the tape recorder. She would dance for the baby, and show her how to turn her hands in the air, a gesture implying dance, and often taught to little girls. Mina would tell me the stories from the films she knew. When I first heard her own story of her mother and her birth, I understood that, from a probable lack of knowledge of her family background, she had fabricated an account filled with motifs and themes from the movie heroes and heroines she identified with. It was her open love of dancing and movie stories, and her ability to dance at parties, and her gay laughter and lightheartedness which gained Mina the low reputation she had. In the Pashtun code of behavior, all these are considered shameful in women, and are severely reprimanded.

Pashto constitutes, beyond the language, both honor and modesty in a complex system of morality. In this Pashto, where behavior is rooted in maintaining honor and reputation, it is also courted by the persistent fear of being shamed. Where reputation is at stake, concern for how others perceive one's words and actions dominates. For women, honor is established by acknowledging and presenting life as a series of hardships, or *ghams*. *Gham* is a word often used in Pashto, meaning sadness, suffering, grief, and distress, as the more tangible phenomenon of hardship, or cause for the worry or grief. Women's honor is found in modesty, restraint, timidity, and in patience with *gham*. And these qualities are enacted through verbal and physical behavior.

For Pashtuns, language and behavior are linked to honor and reputation, and as such are highly scrutinized. Laughter, dancing and singing are strongly prohibited in women's Pashto. So the lighthearted cheerfulness I appreciated in Mina was precisely what other women found so unacceptable in her. In speaking to me of her, they often called her a *dema* in lowered voices. These are a class of barbers and entertainers of very low status, and are considered to have loose morals.

Mina was the only Pashtun woman of her kind I would ever meet. She seemed afraid of no one and of nothing. She argued violently when she didn't like something, but she could also get her way with a smile. She knew that Pashtun men can be abusive and lack all respect where women on their own are concerned, and so she was always on her guard and highly suspicious. She drew this parallel of single womanhood between us, and frequently felt she had to fight for me. She could abuse, but she could also defend from abuse. She defended herself, and at times extended her protective instincts to me also. This came out particularly when we were first setting up house in a village and making arrangements for water or other daily necessities, or when we were shopping together and she did not think I was driving a hard enough bargain.

It was this rebellion against abuse that I admired so much in Mina. And because I admired it, I was stubborn to the harsh criticism addressed to her, and to me for keeping her. Merely by having to work, a Pashtun woman destroys her status and reputation which formerly lay in the fact that she was provided for. She can no longer remain in the safety of home, but must struggle to work in the public domain, vulnerable to abuse because she has no male to protect her. She has no man whose honor sits over her, and therefore she has no status or identity, for a woman's identity lies entirely in her men folk. This shows up in a number of life stories of women who were widowed. In one such story, when the woman's husband died, his brothers offered to marry her. She had a choice between, in her words, "laying myself open to them"or losing everything and leaving, an abandoned woman. Her choice to reject her in-laws' offer of protection and leave was interpreted by people who later heard the story as being the choice of an evil woman. In their opinion, she should have remained with her brothers-in-law.

The feeling of helplessness when faced with the root belief in gender roles concerning honor and reputation, and consequently any part of the cultural system, explains why women turn with anger against any other woman who manages to defy the system and continue to function in it independently. Such was the case with Mina, who found herself, due to barrenness, relegated to the position of less favored older wife kept for housework, while her husband took a younger wife for the position of childbearing and companionship. This woman, the only one I have met among Pashtuns who rebelled, left of her own volition, found her way from the village to the city, and began working one job after another in Peshawar. Outside the city, in rural Pashtun areas, however, she encountered tremendous hostility, and other women even denied her ethnic identity. How could she, with her joyful disposition, stamina, and lack of fear for her reputation, be Pashtun? She could boast the ability to reject a domestic situation she found abusive and to defend herself, an ability to challenge the traditional figures of authority who took it for granted that they could contain her in the slot they created for her as an economically deprived woman without a man. And because of this ability she was insulted and labeled, by women as well as men, as a *dema*.

The sad part of the story is the price Mina paid for her strength and independence. She created an exile for herself, a total social rejection. The angry condemnation she received, and the refusal to admit her into the community of Pashtuns, could be interpreted as a sign of latent envy on behalf of the rural women who could not tolerate her. They reacted with horrified helplessness to the thought of losing their own honor and protection, as Mina had lost hers by leaving her difficult domestic situation and asserting her independence.

Once, Mina had some gold jewelry she had long been wanting to melt down and make earrings from. So when we were living in Madyan, a mountain village in Swat, known for its exceptional gold, she told me one day that she had to consult with me about a special buy for herself. She had been putting aside her salary to buy a television and a VCR, but now she had seen some earrings she desired. "They cost two thousand rupees,' - that was three months' wages she had been saving – "but then, you can't find this quality of gold down in the valley." She was seeking my advice.

I told Mina that in three more months she would again have two thousand rupees, but that Swati gold could only be found in Swat, and we would have moved elsewhere in three months. That decided her, and she announced triumphantly that I would have to celebrate her new purchase with a party. Perhaps, she suggested, I could hire a VCR and some movies for an evening. She would cook up a good meat dish and we would invite friends and neighbors.

I then asked Mina where she had seen these extraordinary earrings. "At Talimena's house." I had known Talimena since 1978, and was very close to her entire family. "They are selling her wedding jewelry so that her husband can buy himself a ticket to Saudi Arabia to work." I had heard of this happening before, where a woman's wedding jewelry, which is ostensibly entirely hers, is appropriated by her husband for his own use. Mina took it for granted, or at least did so now in order to justify her own motives. "This is our Pakistani custom," she added as she noticed my face darken. "If a man has the chance to go to Saudi, he sells his land, his cows and goats. Some even sell their wives."

I told Mina I sensed a great injustice being done, and we spent several days discussing the issue. My ethical position, particularly in view of my relationship with Talimena, did not allow me to sanction the deal, although I told Mina she should do as she pleased. After all, if she did not buy the earrings, someone else would. But I added that she could not count on me to celebrate the event with any joy. The jewelry belongs to the dowry a bride brings from her parents' house. It is hers to rely on in case of divorce. I reminded Mina of a man we both knew in Madyan who had sold his wife's jewelry in order to buy a tape recorder.

Mina's response to this was scorn. "Intelligent women take their precautions and store their jewelry in safe keeping with someone else. Husbands always ask for it eventually, and if the wife doesn't agree, then they argue, and he finally takes it by force. He has no right to it, but he takes it anyway."

89

She went on to explain that she had protected her jewelry immediately upon reaching her husband's village as a new bride by entrusting it to a local wealthy landlord with his promise that he would never give it to anyone but her. Mina felt no pity for women who were "not smart enough to look after their own interests," and if she could purchase a beautiful pair of earrings, it did not matter that they were usurped goods of a friend who had not thought to protect them.

I asked Mina if her husband had ever tried to take her jewelry from her.

"Has he ever?! At first he tried to say that what was mine was his, and what was his was mine. I said, "No, that's not yours; that's entirely mine." He wrote up a paper whereby I was giving him my jewelry, and then he dragged me and forced my thumb over it as my signature. I went to the village landlord with whom I'd entrusted my jewelry. They were all on my side. I told them no matter what, to hold on to that jewelry. It's still with them."

In the end, my opinion mattered to Mina, and she did not buy the earrings, and we remained close friends with that family, visiting the women almost daily. A few days later, Mina decided to buy a quantity of local gold, melt it down with her own gold necklace, and have a pair if spectacular earrings made of the combination. She announced to me and everyone else in our area her plan to go to a village goldsmith on her next day off. At first no one took her seriously, because in rural Pashtun areas, woman seldom ever set foot in the market, and certainly not in the goldsmith's shop. That is an errand a man runs for his wife, sisters, mother, or other womenfolk. As she talked about this excursion and planned it, our neighbors and friends would tease her, and then speak slanderously of her to me. Then, on her next day off, Mina left for the Madyan village bazaar.

When she told the smith what she wanted, he smiled in business-like fashion and suggested she leave the necklace with him. He would have it ready the next day. Mina knew full well the habits of goldsmiths who, when melting gold, replace a portion of it with a lesser grade of gold. She also knew that a goldsmith would have no scruples cheating an ignorant woman in this way. But this was her wedding jewelry, and she knew it was a pure gold, so she replied with her full-cheeked smile, "Oh, I couldn't do that. The gold of my necklace is of such poor quality, and you have such fine gold up here. It would be a shame for you to mistakenly add your high quality gold to what I have. I'll stay and watch." Like many Pashtun women, Mina knew her way around gold.

She returned from the village that night beaming like a child, bursting with pride over her conquest and accomplishment. We heard the story repeatedly over the next weeks, and our admiration of the new jewelry was solicited daily.

Mina had many qualities which made her unique in Pashtun culture. It was these qualities I admired despite how people defamed her for them. Some nights after dinner and after Lawangina was asleep, I did nott feel up to my usual night hours of work, so she and I would talk together. One such night she told me the following story about one of her many jobs in Peshawar.

One time I just told a woman, "Sister,
  Find me some work in the hospital."
Now, that woman said, "Sister,
  You'll have to give me some bribe money."
I did,
  And gave her 200 rupees bribe money.
   I gave her 200 rupees bribe money.

Now, God Almighty is great.
  I had no faith in myself,
   But I had faith in God.
On the twenty-second day, that woman told me,
  "Come, let's go to the hospital."

I went to the hospital.
Now, all the women were going around bare-headed.
  And I said to that woman,
   "Sister, I have faith in God Almighty.
    Just show me how to make two of those eye bandages,
     Those plasters.
      I'll make the third one myself."
She lay down one cloth.
  She patted down the cotton.
   Then she covered it with a thin gauze,
    And made two sets.
     And with the third set, well...

Then I took the scissors in my hand.
  But the hospital scissors were crooked.
And when I put my fingers to those scissors,
    Now blood fell from my fingers down to my elbow right here.
      And I made that bandage.
      I made that bandage.
        The bandage went into the basket.
The man looked at it and was very pleased.
    He told me, "You'll begin work in four days.
      800 rupees. And 8 more.
        808 rupees.

Then, when I came home that day
  I got to thinking, "Great God,
    I'm going to work in that hospital.
      I'll be employed.
Now, I have no friends or relatives there.
  I have no one to shame.
But my husband has many cousins.
  He has many friends and relatives.
    And they'll say...
      When they come, then they'll say,
        "So-and-so's wife is now working here."
Many of our village folk come:
  Cloth dyers
    Shoemakers,
      Landlords,
        Farmers,
          Potters.
Everyone comes,
  And all will see me."

Now respect for my husband was very dear to me.
  800 rupees were not dear to me.
I thought, "I live in my own house.
  And no village folk look at me.
    And no relatives or strangers look at me.
      I don't even show my house to my own village folk.
And what are the village folk?

All the women are related to my trouser hem (mother-in-law),
    Or to my turban (husband).
But I have no one besides myself."

Now, I thought about all this.
    And I will remain cautious for my husband's sake.
        But let it be.
            God will make thing alright.
Now I am a million times thankful to God.
    For I have no difficulties.
        I worked five years in Kiani Saeb's house.
            And I knew myself well.
                And God Almighty has given me everything.
Now I am with an Angrez Bibi.
    God is generous.
    I am a million times thankful to God.

    Mina's discontent began when we moved from the city of Peshawar to the rural mountain village of Madyan in the Swat Valley. Here, in our stone house with a mud and wood roof, we weren't even inside the village, but quite a distance above it, with only a steep path connecting us. There were several other houses up there, including our landlord, Moambar's. His was a large house and courtyard, with two annexes built specifically as rental units. Formerly, they had been rented to foreigners, but since the flow of young Western travelers had ceased and the Russians had invaded Afghanistan, they were now mostly rented to Afghan refugees fleeing the summer heat of Peshawar. Ours was an independent unit with a covered verandah on which we cooked, entertained, ate, and spent most of our time. We looked out onto the village in the valley below, and the snow-covered peaks on the other side. There were two rooms, each with its door opening onto the verandah. Mina slept in one room, where we also stored food and an extra bed where I would sleep if we ever had male guests. The other room was for Lawangina and me, and was where I stored my computer, taping equipment, papers and files.

    The landlord's family had been close friends of mine since 1978, when I had first met and stayed with them. The oldest son, Moambar, had from the start been a valuable informant in my research, mostly due to his good English and his willingness to speak openly about anything I asked him.

As my linguistic skills grew over the years, I also became very close with the women of his house: his mother, wife, brothers' wives and daughter.

Although we had a closed-in outhouse, we had no running water. Once a day, our landlord's pump came on, and we could fill our pots and buckets from his tank for the day. Diapers and baby baths required the most water. Mina and I would carry buckets back and forth from the tank to the house, filling all the vessels, while a child from next door would sit with Lawangina, who did not understand the daily commotion. We had to do it fast while the pump was on.

Mina considered the living situation below her standards, and often argued with the landlord's family. She also found it too strenuous to climb up or down the steep path between the house and the village, especially as it was often muddy from rain. So she refused to shop for groceries, which she had always done in Peshawar, enjoying the outing in the bazaar.

I began to feel Mina's discontent shortly after our arrival in this village, and it was not only due to the work load, which had obviously increased with the lack of facilities. Mina had become very possessive of her relationship with me, and spoke of me proudly to everyone, claiming, "Bibi has only one daughter, called Lawangina. She is in my arms night and day. And Bibi has adopted me as her mother. And I have adopted the Angrez Bibi as my daughter. And she tells me everything." Mina often used these words when talking about her work with me to other people. In Peshawar, she had me almost to herself. I stayed at home working most days, or else went to an office or to the university. Sometimes friends came to visit. Mina liked all my city friends, although several of them had told me after visiting my house that Mina had asked them to run interference and ask me to raise her salary. They regarded this with abomination and suggested I replace her.

I had been among Pashtuns for almost a decade, and was quite familiar with people's attempts to slander and defame each other to me. Hence I disregarded many of these warnings for months, and, remaining amused, persisted in defending Mina. But only a week after we had been in Madyan the slander grew worse and began coming from both directions. I had already seen this happen before when we had moved from the city to another Pashtun village for a short time. She intensely disliked the new place, and treated everyone like an enemy who was threatening to break her and my relationship. And villagers also perceived her as an evil force seeking to exploit me and hinder my work. Pashtuns also regarded her smiling, cheery lightheartedness as shameful.

Not only did the women from Moambar's house argue with Mina and repeatedly tell me that she was worthless and dishonorable, but Mina would tell me how I was being cheated by them. I did not want to lose Moambar's family's friendship, nor did I want to lose Mina's service. She and I argued increasingly, however, and she began threatening to leave. She had begun washing laundry for a single male foreigner renting a room on the other side of Moambar's house. Some days she would sweetly and plaintively say she was doing it out of the goodness of her heart, and other days she would rage that the service had gone on gratis long enough, and it was time for the man to pay up. Moambar's wife and mother pleaded with me to make her stop on the grounds that she was working for me and should not show her disloyalty by working elsewhere simultaneously. What worried me was that the time she put into these extra chores was time taken from my daughter. She became livid with I asked her to stop.

Mina spent much of the time in Moambar's house so Lawangina could play with the children there and she would have company. When the first of the month came and I paid her, Mina ran screaming to them that I was cheating her on her salary. When we had arrived, she had announced to them that I was paying her three hundred rupees more than I actually did pay her. Now she went waving the money to them and accusing me of not paying up. A commotion ensued involving us and all the women from Moambar's house, and Moambar was sent for from his shop in the village to mediate the dispute.

Mina had a particular sore spot for Moambar, whose family I had been close with for over a decade now. He would come over after dinner at night and talk with me. I would ask him about people, about linguistic phenomena I had encountered that day in my translations, or about social transactions I had not clearly understood. Once, on such an evening, Mina suddenly shot out of her room and ran to Moambar's house, where everyone was already asleep. She screamed for all to come out and witness that the two of us were sitting up late together at nights talking so no one could sleep. It was Moambar's wife who calmed her down and reassured her it was alright, that we had been friends for years and that I was like his own sister. But to Mina, Moambar continued to present a major threat to her relationship with me, and she persisted in trying to turn us against each other by making up stories to create anger and suspicion.

As the quarrels between Mina and me grew to verbal fights which the neighbors had to interfere in, both of us began to speak of Mina's departure. On several occasions she threatened to leave, but when I told her to pack up and go ahead, her anger turned to tears and pleas. She cried that she was my mother and I her daughter, that she only wanted my success, and that she wouldn't leave without creating a public scandal and ruining Moambar's life here forever. Meanwhile, however, I was looking for someone else in the village to replace her. I was questioning my own ability to react rationally to her, and often found myself trembling with rage. I was losing weight and was perpetually anxious.

In one of our disputes, I accused her of taking advantage of my friends. The women of Moambar's family made ornate wool braids which Moambar sold in his shop. These are a popular Pashtun women's hair accessory, and Mina had commissioned a large number of these to take as gifts to her family, but she had never paid for them. She had also had Moambar's sister-in-law make her six sets of clothes with her sewing machine, and had never paid her for them. When I reminded Mina that she was far wealthier than these people and that she had no right to take advantage of my friends this way, she yelled out that she pissed on my friends, and that she was here to make a profit where she could, and that included off my friends. Moreover, she refused ever to prepare tea or meals for any poor villagers who came to the house. She would entertain my more affluent guests in Peshawar, and would even dance for them, she insisted. But she would have nothing to do with these poorer rural people.

Mina's base contempt for people poorer than herself was a result of her having struggled so hard. She had sacrificed her honor in order to make her wealth and achieve what she had in the working world. When I asked her how she felt about being better off than the women I dealt with daily, she responded:

I am rich because I've burned myself,
   I've given myself trouble.
      And night after night I said nothing.
      And day after day I said nothing.
When my employer would call me, "Mina!"
   Then I'd say, "Yes, Saeb."
He'd tell me, "Get such-and-such ready."
   I'd prepare it at once and give it to him.

Now, God gave me good money in Peshawar.
   I earned well.
      If someone told me to polish shoes,
         I would polish shoes.

96

If someone told me to wash two suits of clothes,
  I would wash two suits of clothes,
    And take money for it.
There's nothing I wouldn't do.
  Except steal.
And God Almighty has saved me from prostitution.
For the rest, I've done all honest work.

Now there's a proverb:
  "The face is pretty or the behavior is good.
    The work is good, or the moon is pretty."
If a woman is ugly but her work is good,
  People will pay her for her work.
  No one gives money just in the name of God.

The day after this discussion I returned to the house in the afternoon to meet with the most violent and drawn out confrontation I had ever been involved in. At some points I had to hold myself back from laughing at a distance. As I approached the house, I was met by Moambar's mother and father, who counseled me. "We've heard you're looking for another ayah. Don't do this. Do what you must with Mina, but come to an agreement and keep her. We'll talk to her, too. You'll never find anyone in the village who'll do as much as she does. Our village women will all leave you at night, and steal from you. Get rid of her when you return to Peshawar if you want, but you brought her here, and it would be very bad if you sent her back."

Although Moambar's mother argued incessantly with Mina, and his father often berated me for keeping her, they were now obviously doing their best to have me keep her. In bits and pieces from the younger women in Moambar's house, and from his relatives in the village, I leaned the underlying reason behind their urging me to keep Mina. He and his parents had a severe dislike and mistrust of the villagers, and had moved up in the mountain specifically to escape and live free of worry from spying and gossip. The thought that I should bring a woman from the village, who would then gossip about them below, was more intolerable than putting up with Mina for several months. I had to respect this, although the price for all concerned was heavy.

As they were speaking with me outside the compound at the top of the path from the village, women of the family slowly emerged, with children on their hips, and Mina also joined us, with Lawangina in her arms. I took the baby, and in no time, Moambar's father, the only male there, became a target in the middle as voices were raised and Mina and I shot our gripes about each other at him. She pleaded that she was poor and thoroughly devoted to me, and would throw herself in the river at my command. And I accused her of lying, of insulting me and my friends, and of threatening to leave so that I had to make other arrangements.

After this first set of angry allegations, things quieted down slightly as Mina broke into sobs as always, and the older parent figures acted to calm us down. The entire crowd moved together into the main house, where I fed my daughter while we sat together. I was still angry, and had not yet finished with Mina, but also knew that if I said anything in front of this crowd she would only start her crying again and plead devotion and innocence. We left it at that and came home, where I calmly announced to Mina that she had to decide one way or another if she wanted to leave, because I had someone else lined up to replace her. In tears, Mina pleaded that she had decided from the start that she was staying with me.

Our discussion ended abruptly because Lawangina began crying. I took her on my lap and was writing in my room when I heard loud angry voices coming from next door. Moambar's sister-in-law and mother were yelling at each other and at Mina in Mina's room. I went over, but felt grateful that I was not expected to participate in this one. I could not have competed with the trio in its shouting match of insults and accusations. I stood against the wall, holding my daughter close to me and whispering to her.

Badera, Moambar's sister-in-law, and her mother-in-law had had a hostile relationship ever since I had first met them. Each one spoke pejoratively of the other, and they were rarely seen together although they were neighbors. Now Badera was yelling at Mina and accusing her of slandering everyone and hindering good relations with her malicious gossip. Moambar's mother was yelling at Badera and accusing her of enticing me to get rid of Mina. Mina was yelling to defend herself against the allegation that she had not paid for the clothes she had had Badera make.

I was still standing silently with Lawangina in my arms, wanting to show support for Badera, whom I considered a friend and whom I knew was snubbed by the entire family, when in walked Moambar. He began yelling at all three of them. First, he yelled at his mother to shut up. Then he yelled at Mina to pay up and stay out of people's business. He also told her that she was nothing to them, and that the only reason they all tolerated her was for my sake. Then he yelled at Badera for even being there, and he chased everyone away. Mina now accused Moambar of being at the center of everything, and of slandering her to me behind her back. He accused her of not being a decent Muslim because she massaged the English man when he was half dressed. The yelling and crying went on while we filled all our pots with water, because the pump had come on. In the end, to put things to rest, I agreed to give Mina half of the raise she had allotted herself, and she agreed to take half.

This was only one of several similar incidents that occurred between us during the months spent in Madyan. Each time it happened, I felt more involved in Pashtun family politics. One of Mina's strongest claims against me which kept emerging in these confrontations was that I was not a proper *Angrez*, or foreigner. "Real *Angrez* don't understand us or what we do. They just sit in luxurious offices and houses, pay out high salaries and let us do what we want. Your problem is that you're not a real *Angrez*."

As far as Mina was concerned, I, in my ethnographic capacity as participant observer, had violated a very deeply rooted image of foreigner-hood. Although she wanted to remain working for me because I paid her higher wages than most Pakistani employers, and no other foreigner would hire her because she spoke no English, she wanted me to abide by the image she had of the foreign employer. She could not tolerate our life in the villages, and became determined to have me return to the city. The little ways in which she had begun coming between me and my friends like Moambar's family grew worse. People in Madyan began questioning me suspiciously about my work, and I discovered she was telling them that her employer was a highly paid CIA agent. Mina told people in the village that I wore twenty to thirty microphones hidden under my clothes, and that my objective was to tape women's voices and then have them broadcast on public radio. This would shame them all and cause a number of deaths, as pashto strictly forbids that the live voice of a woman should be heard beyond the walls of her own house. Mina was furthermore sowing fear among my informants by declaring that I was an enemy of Muslims, and that my work was ultimately to destroy Muslim ideals and values.

Mina knew exactly how best to affect me and my work in the strongest manner. She knew how to stimulate people's deepest fears and shatter the confidence which I had spent years building up. Fortunately, the people I had known the longest would not hear this from her, but I found doors closed where it concerned more recent friends, or people I did not know personally.

Our domestic disputes grew worse, and now Mina threatened that I could never dismiss her, that she would come after me and ruin my life and my research. For Moambar's sake, I said nothing and we remained together throughout my four months in Madyan. But as soon as we returned to the city, I fired Mina and took on a new ayah. Almost immediately, Pashtun friends and neighbors began telling me things about Mina that they had hesitated to tell me before, adding that they had not felt they could tell me while I was employing her and, by the rules of that relationship, owed her protection. Now they openly criticized my choice of an ayah in Mina. They reproached me for not having been a better judge of character when they had all known right from the first meeting that she was a "rotten woman." And when I hired my second ayah, and my household settled down more peaceably and harmoniously, I was congratulated for having learned and understood about acceptability in women's pashto.

As difficult as my time with Mina was, I felt I still owed it to her to reveal her story, our story together. What had attracted me to her in the beginning - her strength of character, her ability to challenge abuse and assert herself as a woman in this culture - was precisely what society condemned in her and what it held against me for condoning.

Bus Depot

VIII. BUS RIDES – TWO TALES

B elow are two stories of memorable bus ride experiences.

I.

I was late leaving Peshawar, hoping to arrive in Madyan, a village in the northern Swat Valley, in one day. On the local bus leaving Peshawar, I was seated on the last bench next to an old woman and her great grandson, and a young girl working in the city and off to spend Friday with her folks in Mardan. It was great there in the back seat by the window, well sheltered. We would laugh and tease the rude fare collector. "Hide your face," my neighbor would tell me with a grin, or "Don't answer anything," she'd warn when he snapped a comment I clearly didn't understand.

The fare collector's job is to yell. All day he yells to the driver to stop or go. He yells across the bus for fares he can't physically reach. He yells things to people sitting up front. He yells out the bus's destination every time the bus approaches a village and drives through it. So, even when he's not trying, he yells hoarsely.

Mardan is a major stop on the way north. It was unbearably hot on this July day, and I was soaked through to the bus's plastic seat. Women do not leave the bus in transit, but must remain patiently seated in the stagnating 110 degrees, wrapped tightly in their veils of honor, and buying cold drinks or whatever from vendors who mill around bus windows holding up their wares: roasted corn, bananas, guavas, sugar cane cubes, sodas, bread and grilled meat patties, candies, cakes, even car-sickness horse pills. "Ice water, ice water, ice water," yelled a young boy limping around the outside

103

of the bus with a pail of water and a tin cup he held up to our windows. When his pail emptied, he went to the nearest creek to refill it.

No one stood still for a moment, despite the heat. No one, that is, except the women, keeping nose and mouth covered by dirty, sweaty veils, in hopes that the bus would soon take off and create some breeze. That was the only thought preoccupying them: "Let's move!" But in the midst of all this bustle, our bus seemed to have trouble leaving. The driver raced his engine and sounded his horn, moved the bus forward a few inches threateningly and backed up again, but his bus still would not fill, and the rule is that a bus cannot leave the depot until every seat is occupied. However, it is not the driver's job to fill it, and his fare collector had left to go eat rather than drag clients on the bus and yell out its destination. So we sat a long time.

In Mardan, the fare collector moved me to a seat over the back wheel well of the bus, with my knees cramped up under my chin. The sweat, heat, dust, smells, bodies crushing each other, all filled the bus entirely, so that there was no hope of seeing any scenery if I didn't keep my nose glued to my little rip in the colored paper covering the window. I spent the next five hours there without moving. A corpulent woman with her ample veil and child were seated next to me, squeezing me in even more with her generous hips.

The seat over the wheel well sat just in front of the rear door, where the fare collector usually stood by default when he wasn't busy. During the ride, as I was trying to see through the rip in the window paper and watch the mountains, I had felt his hand touch my side. Standing in the rear doorway, he had slipped his hand outside the door and in through my window. I immediately turned my back to the window and felt enraged. I discovered this was a common practice and after that, I never traveled without a knife to gently stab at wandering, grabbing hands.

The joy was in reaching the mountains and feeling the air cool progressively, offering relief in blowing through my dirty sticky clothes.

II.

Peshawar to Dera Ismail Khan by government bus: 35 rupees. One night in a double room in the Al-Habib Hotel: 25 rupees. Dinner of meats and radishes: 8.5 rupees. Two boxes of famous Dera sweets: 20 rupees. An anonymous ride through the tribal area of Waziristan: priceless.

I had decided, for my second trip to Quetta, to take the bus through the tribal area. I had taken the train through the Punjab and Sindh the first time and it had proved a long painful voyage. Eighty or so women, children and babies had sat packed on benches in one compartment, unable to move for three days, throwing all the trash on the floor at our feet as we ate. It was on that ride I had learned to dissociate my feet from the rest of my body. Although I had paid for a birth, I was lucky if I could hold on to just my seat throughout the ride. I had sucked on lemons through the whole trip so as not to take in liquids and hence lose my seat if I had to leave it for the toilets. Women and children had been shoved in through the windows onto our laps at station stops because the doors were so packed tight. It had definitely not been a pleasant experience, and I decided that if travel must be long and difficult I could at least make it enjoyable with some beautiful scenery to look at.

The bus ride cost more than the train, including all the hotel and meal costs, but was well worth it. It followed the western belt in turban country, through the barren arid mountains and passes of the Pashtun and Baluch tribal lands. The train had taken me to lands of Punjab and Sindh that felt foreign and uncomfortable, from Urdu spoken on board to the way people were dressed in the countryside. I had to admit my weakness for the familiar. Among Pashtuns I felt secure, even if removed.

Leaving Peshawar, we were three women on the bus, and the other two were with men. I had started out on a seat in the back of the bus, but obviously, no man would sit by me and the bus was crowded. And since it could not leave with an unoccupied seat, I changed places with an old man accompanying one of the women. Just my luck - she took up three quarters of the bench, leaving me with one buttock falling off, and both legs in the isle due to her satchel, immovably heavy, at my feet. For four and a half hours I was compelled to concentrate with all my energy on just clinging on, grabbing the seat in front for support without touching the man seated in it. I braced myself with one foot stuck out across the isle, taking care not to let my knee touch the man sitting there, trying to nudge myself back on the seat a bit after every sharp turn where I'd nearly fall off. The turns were many as we were mostly on the sinuous road crossing the Kohat Pass, and then another range of hills after Kohat. A certain intimacy is formed between women in such a situation. At the lunch stop, she and I went to the fields together to squat and pee under our veils. But we couldn't talk much, as she was from Banu and I could barely understand her without much thought, which delayed my comprehension and reactions beyond the possibility of coherent conversation. But the peeing excursion brought us together in childish laughter.

The third woman on the bus, sitting with her man in the front seat, did not budge, eat or drink a thing brought to her window by her brother. I admired her, seeing only the back of her feet in red sandals. I ate nothing, either, figuring it was safer, and also disgusted by my bench partner who ate a bread and some fried fish, and who seemed to expand over the seat with every bite.

At Banu, my neighbor got off and I climbed into the single seat just in front of the other woman. I was finally alone, with a whole seat to myself, the front seat, so that there was no worry of anyone turning around to stare at me. I relaxed every muscle, letting the sun filter in warmly through the glass window. In fact, it was unbearably hot, and I'd come dressed for the snow and freezing weather of Quetta in January. I could not turn around to speak to the woman in the seat behind me except when the bus emptied of men, which happened briefly at Banu, and again at a village some seventy miles from Dera Ismail Khan for late afternoon prayers.

Seeing that I was alone, the fare collector had taken charge of me, offering to bring tea, bread or fruit to my window at every stop. Naturally, I had declined each offer, fearing a lack of toilet facilities later. Now, again, he and the girl's brother came to our respective windows to enquire if we would drink tea or eat fruit. Both of us refused. When the bus stopped for prayers, I turned and asked her if she would like to go "to the fields." She had withheld herself all day, not daring to go alone or to ask anyone. She would have remained like that, wordless, motionless, until a woman came to her. Her brother walked ahead, leading us to a field outside the village where we could squat in peace.

A woman's fate on the bus is a hard one. She must sit quietly, squeezed in, sweating, possibly vomiting discreetly under the stench of her own veil. She cannot utter a word, turn her head to look at anything, or get up to stretch her legs. If a male relative is not there to cater to her needs, she just remains a noiseless statue glued to the seat until arrival. No one addresses or even glances at her. I sat according to custom, not wanting to draw attention to myself, my veil properly wrapped and held in my teeth so I could read. I only climbed off twice all day, always accompanied by another woman. I smoked one cigarette when the men had all left the bus, which I had sent the fare collector to buy for me.

I had learned from observing Pashtun women in public places, that the more authoritative a woman acts here, the more respect she gains. If I didn't act hesitant or friendly, no one would with me, either. But I was tired after this first long day, and not in the mood to be demanding or to fight for my rights. In Banu, the fare collector had told me the ongoing bus would not leave till the next day, and he sent me to a hotel in a bicycle-pulled rickshaw. I was apprehensive at first to enter a strange hotel in a strange town alone. The manager, seeing all my bundles, scoffed at me, making fun of me to his mates in the hotel office. But as soon as I took charge and began demanding to be served a meal in my room and be woken up in the morning, he lost his salacious grin, lowered his eyes, and ordered everyone out while I signed the register. He asked all sorts of questions before he finally asked if I were a foreigner.

It still was not time to relax. Now I had to deal with the hotel boy. When he first showed me to the room, the electricity went out. I hesitated a moment, not sure whether to proceed or not, and noticed the shadow of his hand come near me. That decided me, and I marched out to the courtyard, complaining in the strong, high-pitched voice I'd learned to use, that I'd stand there until someone brought a candle, and that I refused to remain in an unlit room. The young man at once became subservient, and rushed to get a candle. The more I demanded from him, the less he even looked at me, but lowered his eyes, and answered, "Ji."

"I want to be woken up at six a.m., you hear?," I started.. "Now, bring me some dinner: ground meat, bread and a pot of tea, you understand? Not one or two cups, but a big pot. Make it mixed tea." I ate dinner and then rang for him again: "What's happened to the tea? Hurry up!" Then I rang again, after he had come and gone several times with the trays, the bill, and the change. "Listen now, run over to the nearest sweet shop and get me two boxes of Dera sweets. And don't try to steal from me because I know the prices, you hear?" The sweets from this town are renowned in Pakistan, and I figured I would bring some to my friends in Quetta.

When the boy finally returned with the sweets, it was to ask if I needed anything else. I said no, and with his eyes still averted, he nodded his head to the side and went away. Exhausted, I felt proud. Perhaps I was learning to behave as a woman here. I remembered the warnings of an anthropology professor from Peshawar University when I had first arrived in Peshawar: "Don't try to be American in Pakistan. You won't survive."

I was up and gone at six the following morning, after a restless night during which I'd eaten one of the boxes of sweets. I had my rickshaw driver stop and buy me two more boxes. The early morning ride was quiet. Dera is a desert town, where the dominant sound is voices and roosters rather than motor scooters with broken mufflers. When we pulled into the bus station, I was surprised to see the quietest, emptiest station ever. The vast closed-in courtyard had three buses in it, empty, and a few blanketed men standing around. The bus to Lorelei would not leave till two o'clock. I was obliged to take a room, one of the many green doors giving on to the main courtyard, which must be the only station in Pakistan where one hears birds instead of roaring bus engines. At first the manager wanted thirty rupees for the room.

"What?" I retorted. "Don't be stingy, you infidel. State the correct price!" I had to be on my guard even before dawn, but it paid off, and for fifteen rupees I was brought to a charming little open courtyard, walled in by white plaster over brick, a brick floor with a sewer and canal running through the middle, and an outhouse with a clean drainage in the corner, and a regular flush system and shower. No hot water, but even winter here is warm enough to stand cold water. A room in the back was furnished with three rope cots and a clean new cotton mattress. This was heaven! For once, I didn't have to sit in the dark, but could have my door open to the warmth outside, and could even sit in my private sunny courtyard.

So, this would be my home until the afternoon. I sent the boy out to get tea and cigarettes, and an old bearded, turbaned, spectacled secretary came to my door with his book to have me register. He was surprised to discover that I knew how to write. He usually had to fill it in for guests, and have them sign with their thumb print. In order not to arouse suspicion or bring in the police who would tell me I couldn't travel this route through tribal area, I wrote in that I was an Iranian student traveling home, and invented a false passport number. Upon hearing this, the old man became especially warm to me and began speaking to me in a broken Persian he had learned while in Afghanistan. Who says a woman can't travel alone here, or go to hotels? I told him not to forget me for the bus, gave him the money get me a ticket to Zhob, where I would change buses, and asked him to come back at noon to bring me some lunch. All this I could never do back home. I could never act with such exigent authority and get away with it. How many people would laugh and respond, "Lady! The coffee shop is right there. Go yourself! I've got my own business to take care of."

As the day progressed, how could I help but be suspicious about this supposed bus depot which accommodated more camels than buses. Not a single bus had come or gone through all day. No one was around. The old white beard had brought me some bread and three chunks of meat in a bowl of oil at noon. The sun had come and gone across my brick courtyard, which was more pleasant than inside the room where the damp floor was covered with orange peels and dry mutton bones. They had made me pay fifteen rupees to keep my face hidden, and thirty rupees for a ticket to Zhob, which I was beginning to suspect was all a farce. I was sure there must be a regular bus station from which buses leave all day. I finally called over to the old guy and exploded, asking if this were really a bus station.

"Yes," he replied. "Don't worry about a thing," he repeated several times, trying to keep me calm and reassured. "I've put you in the front seat just behind the driver. There is another man and woman, also resting in a room. They're going to Quetta and will see you get on the right bus at Zhob. But this bus only travels at night. It takes a short cut through the tribal area and cannot go during the day because of the danger there."

So, the two o'clock was a.m., not p.m. I was disappointed that I would be crossing this particular stretch of land at night, hence unable to see it, but glad that there was no one telling me I couldn't go there. For the hundredth time, I couldn't help thinking that if I conformed to local behavioral expectations, I could enjoy the privilege of traveling safely on my own. Admittedly, had I been traveling as a tourist with other foreigners, we could have seen the bazaar, eaten well and talked to all sorts of interesting people, but in the end we would have taken the long route to Quetta.

We finally did leave at two o'clock in the morning, after I had been pacing diagonally in my room since midnight. I'd fallen asleep right after the evening oil, meat and bread, delivered to my door right after dusk prayers. I had no watch, but I woke up feeling it must be time. I was haunted by the continual sound of bus and truck engines in the distance, but none seemed to come here. For a moment I felt desperate, thinking that the old man would again calm me with promises of leaving at the following two o'clock, and charge me another fifteen rupees for another day, and thus keep me here, making money on my naiveté. I began pacing angrily, loudly, rehearsing all my possible ripostes to his smiles. I almost expected to see daylight at any moment. Then, just as I was overtaken with sleep and lay down again, the hotel boy pounded on the door to wake me. We were leaving.

We drove through tribal Waziristan all day, though the road could barely be called a road, and it took us over twelve hours to cover 125 kilometers (not even 90 miles). At least, it was a road not many cars could get by on, and in fact, I saw no cars. We crossed paths occasionally with trucks or buses, with small-looking heads peering out from small front panes. Behind their tightly framed front wind shields, these drivers can push on some twenty to thirty hours at a time without interruption.

Actually, it is a road with no place to stop: there is only desert, mountains of wild shades and stripes, canyons and layered ridges, all seeming so untamed. I stopped counting the rivers we had to cross, wondering each time if this road was used at all when the rains fell and the rivers swelled up. Often it became just a maze of cratered tracks. You took your pick and hoped your vehicle would get through in one piece. At other times there were large stones thrown together and spaced apart, reminding me of the way I had built a pier once as a child. This had to be the worst thing for the bus tires. But it was the most incredible landscape I had ever been through, inspiring notions of timelessness and emptiness even more than the dusty arid stretches of Afghanistan I had driven through. It was impossible to do anything all day but gaze out the window, abandoning myself to it all. Even my book seemed mundanely silly next to this beauty.

By early afternoon, I found myself once again relegated to the dark damp cold of a teahouse back room at the Zhob bus station, a room tinier than before, with no permission to exit into the main teahouse, and only two paces' space for any sort of exercise to warm up with or stretch my legs. Would I ever reach Quetta? I was depressed with these dark, cold, mice-ridden cave-like cells I was always locked away in for protection. But I could seek no sympathy for my despair: it had been my choice. On the contrary, I had to pay twenty rupees for my cell, more than I had paid for a sunny courtyard, toilet and shower!

This time I was between the front tea house, from where the usual chorus of shouting male voices wafted through the widely spaced wood boards of my door and window, and the back garden and outhouse, where I allowed myself to enjoy tea in the sun upon arriving. But Sardar Khan, the teahouse boy, was quick to come out with his concerned look and urge me to sit inside my room. "There are men, you know. They come and go from tea to the outhouse. You sit in your room and shut the door, and no one will bother you at all. Tonight there will be many men here, but I will sleep right across your doorway."

So I was condemned by my sex, once again, to remain cold and hidden in the dark, only listening to the laughing male voices as they passed time by the warm hearth drinking little bowls of green tea. Sardar Khan had taken me into his protection and responsibility, and he would protect and defend me as long as I continued to respect my end of the code, remain in my room and have to do with no one but him for anything. If he saw me so much as show my face outside my door, the deal would be off. Oddly enough, I enjoyed being there, feeling anonymous, listening to the chorus of male voices.

Later that night, the tea house, which also served as hotel, filled up outside my door. Fifteen rope cots were lined up side by side in two rows, so that one just climbed over them. Each cot, along with dirty, old, flea-ridden bedding cost five rupees a night. These were the drivers and travelers, talking in loud voices, or bursting out into laughter. They told stories of feuds and revenge killings. One man told about his brother who had been shot by someone, so he roamed all over Waziristan looking for him. When he found him, he shot him once. The bullet did not kill him, though, so he shot him in the face, claiming his revenge was then complete. But the dead man's relatives claim that by laws of revenge, he had the right only to a single shot, and certainly not to mess up his face, so they were now demanding revenge. A big *jerga* with elders from all over had appealed, but there was no stopping these relatives. The man would be killed and the feud would be pursued.

The story that seemed to hold everyone's attention that evening, however, was the recent news event concerning the paid assassin. I was familiar with the story from the Peshawar newspapers some days earlier. I had heard from the Col. Sherif that the custom in the NWFP is that such a person must bring his victim's head to his employer as proof that the job is completed. There had been a long standing feud existing among a certain Pashtun clan whose members are divided now between Afghanistan and Pakistan's NWFP. The feud had been going on for generation, each side respectfully keeping the order of their turns, and it was the Pakistani side's turn to kill one of the Afghan cousins. Haji Saeb, a wealthy drug dealer from the Afridi tribal area, had therefore kept the tradition, but due to the war across the border, he had thought it prudent to hire a professional hit man to do the job. He paid him half in advance, promising the rest once he received the heads of his three cousins. The narrator explained to his spellbound audience how the assassin had been arrested bringing the heads across the Torkham border, hidden amid a bunch of cabbages. His inattentiveness to the blood dripping from his bag as he walked past the customs officials gave him away. I fell asleep listening to other such stories.

When Sardar woke me at three o'clock in the morning to tell me the news, I couldn't have cared less, but felt obliged to manifest utmost worry, like a bride who has to cry at her wedding. "I had to put two men next to you. There are no other women on the bus. Unless, of course, you want to pay for those two seats, besides your own." I didn't. He left and I went back to sleep, not feeling the least bit slighted by the matter. At four o'clock the hotel man woke to have me sign the register a second time, and I asked him for some dry bread, all that I would be eating the entire day. I swallowed it as voraciously as ever and went back to sleep. At six-thirty, the pounding came again at my door. "Hurry up and get your things ready! The bus is waiting." I rushed to pack up, thinking they had perhaps filled the bus and were letting me get on last. No way, and quite the contrary! I climbed on alone and had to sit alone in the cold while the men drank morning tea by the hearth.

They all climbed on at once, each one in turn staring at the single woman, and the seat next to mine was the last to be filled. My veil was completely covering my face. And I was turned to face the window. At least on this trip I wouldn't have someone falling all over me. My neighbor sat upright with his head turned away, both hands folded on his knee farthest from me. Hence we maintained our positions for the first five hours, neither uttering a word. But curiosity piqued me. I had cleared my eyes of my veil so as to enjoy another day of brown barren plains and hills, and tried to espy him in the driver's mirror, as it would have been altogether shocking to look straight at my strange neighbor. All I could see, though, was a dark moustache indicating a young but mature man, and a long shaved narrow chin. The first thing he did utter, after five hours, when I had begun squirming in my seat, was, "I'm not giving you any problem, am I? You have enough room?"

Yes, I thanked him, still not looking, and refraining from the smile which might ordinarily have been given in response to his thoughtfulness. Very slowly, like this, we began, with the next subject being the Pashto story book of Momen Khan and Shiriney I was reading. He was part of a group of six or seven Afghans, having just crossed over the border from their village near Ghazni, leaving their parents, wives, sisters and children over there. They would work in the Quetta area over the three winter months and then return "when the cold, snow, and war were over."

One of the boys from Ghazni asked to see my Pashto book, and he began singing it to those around. These chap books are written in verse with the intent of being sung aloud. Always with my tape recorder on hand, I asked my neighbor to tape it, as I could not move, and had to keep my hands to myself. My turbaned neighbor became mediator for all my conversations after that, and he saw to my needs for that stretch of the journey. Later, the same boy who had sung my book, was singing two-line verses to himself, and I asked if I could tape him. He refused, and stopped singing, claiming his voice was hoarse. But the bus driver, directly behind whom I was sitting, upon hearing the commotion, volunteered to sing a few verses. Wrapped in his blanket, one hand on the wheel and the other holding the recorder up to his mouth, he began a long song. I listened to the roaring Bedford engine, and wondered how any of this would come out on the tape. The driver was from Zhob, and his Waziri accent heavy, so I had trouble understanding, but the interest had caught the attention of all passengers now, and each wanted a turn to sing into the tape recorder. Everyone cheered and encouraged the driver, and my neighbor even nudged me, laughing. He took the recorder from the driver and yelled a verse into it so loud his voice cracked, and his verse was answered by one of his friends. The young Afghans sang a series of modern verses about the war, popular in Ghazni. And so the rest of the ride to Quetta went, with singing almost all the way.

Bird Raising

IX. AZIZA, REFUGEE AND STUDENT

In 1983 I attended a seminar on Pashto literature at the Pashto Academy for a while whenever I was in Peshawar. Professor Khattak presented a figure of great authority, using a voice and reminded me of church preaching. An enormous fan in his classroom made so much noise that his words were all blown behind him before they could travel forward. Twelve chairs were arranged in a semi-circle around his desk. At 9:10 or 9:15, the first students would meander in for the 9:00 class. The class began when everyone had arrived, which usually happened all at once. The men would enter together, followed by four inseparable girls: two from Peshawar, and two from Kabul. They would walk in, looking modest, or timid.

I first met the four women in the hallway when Prof. Khattak was showing me around the Academy and library. They were walking almost in single file, so that when he stopped them to introduce me, they were lined up against the wall, all four of them mute and looking petrified, hugging their books close to their chests. One of these four was Aziza. When Professor Khattak introduced us, he suggested that Aziza could assist me in transcribing my field tapes. During the course of the four years I knew and worked with her, we became friends.

Aziza was twenty-four when I first met her. Her family was from Kandahar, and she had come to Peshawar by way of Quetta in 1980 with them. She had begun studying in the Pashto Department of the University of Peshawar, and was completing her master's when we met. I went one

115

day to meet with her in the Fatimah Jinnah hostel where she was living, and work on some tapes she had agreed to help me transcribe.

The girls' hostel on campus was run more strictly than the most severe girls' boarding school I've ever known. How lucky I felt to be housed with a family and not end up there. It was a strange mélange of Diderot's eighteenth century French convents and of the mysterious, maiden-filled garden descriptions from classical Persian poetry.

I walked for a good hour before finding the Jinnah hostel, as it was removed from anything, and no one I asked seemed to know exactly where it was. It was my last attempt before giving up entirely and going home frustrated. The sky had grown black and the wind had picked up. I bent down to pass through the waist-high metal door carved into the tall gate. Everything was so well enclosed. A young lady could simply disappear behind these iron gates, kept by an armed guard, and no one would ever find her again.

When I walked in, the wind became violent, and a fierce dust storm struck up like it does here in the Fall before the rains arrive. I had to shut my eyes, keeping my face covered with my veil, which blew all over and would not stay in place. How do these girls do it? A narrow passage led me through to the main inner courtyard, where suddenly everything was completely calm. The hostel is shaped like a giant mosque or religious school, with its two-storey arched verandahs circling the enormous interior garden. I was in the precious interior where only girls wearing flowered prints, light veils floating in cross breezes, and long black braids, idly study, play, pass the time until the day they are married to their cousins and in-laws, and start bearing children. I was reminded of the princesses' gardens and maidens I had read about so often in Persian poetry and romances.

Aziza confided with a smile that she was miserable in this hostel. Her brother worked in Islamabad, and her parents were trying to relocate there, so even though they had a house here in Peshawar, in Shahin Town, Aziza was obliged to live in the hostel. She complained of having lost weight, though I perceived her as quite a hefty young woman. "In Kandahar, I was good and fat," she told me, "but here there is nothing to eat and I've lost it all." We sat on the verandah to work. In the garden, girls were strolling by two and threes, never a single one alone, their veils waving stubbornly in the breeze. Not a book in sight, not a single face frowning or strained from tension, frustration or lack of sleep. I saw none of the signs so often associated with university dorm students. Across the garden on the balcony, two girls were idly sitting, their posture enough to calm any human spirit. I felt very girlish, childish sitting there with Aziza.

"These girls will all marry their family and friends," announced Aziza.

"Well, what about yourself?" I asked, sensing her sadness.

"Who do you want me to marry? My family and friends aren't here. They're not Pakistanis."

I invited her to the old city for the next day, to a restaurant for kabab, and she agreed.

Once I left through that tiny metal door, which Aziza could not cross, I at once felt the harshness of the outside world, and welcomed it. I could wipe that lazy smile off my face, and harden my muscles to reality once more. I walked fast with eyes downcast, leaving behind the leisurely stroll of the garden.

We left early the next day, as Aziza's professors did not show up for class, a common occurrence at the Pashto Academy. I had gone to photocopy some materials, but had barely done a single page of translation in the library when the electricity was cut off, another common occurrence one had to tolerate. I was still relatively newly arrived, and had yet to accustom myself to such frustrations.

So, we walked down the quiet lane to Khyber Road and climbed into a white minibus serving as public transportation through town. I admired Aziza's calm self assurance that went well with her domineering build. Once on the minibus, she wasn't about to be crowded, as is the practice with women on the bus. The fare-collector, who also seats everyone, often pushes three to four women in the front seat of a minivan, and God help the one closest to the driver, struggling to keep her legs from being pushed against the stick shift and hand. Aziza yelled right back at the fare-collector when he wanted us to squeeze and make room for a third woman and her two children. All in looking straight ahead, she won her argument, and we were left with the front bench to ourselves. For someone whom I thought sequestered and unable to fend for herself, she certainly proved ostensibly impetuous, a girl who knew her way around and from whom I, on the contrary, had much to learn.

We climbed off at the Iranian center to return some books at their library, and she took out some more on women's rights. As we stood at the desk to check them out, I laughingly asked her what use she could have for them here, and she retorted with that facial expression which in less than half a second seems to snap, "Hush up, what does it matter?" She used that same expression and tone later in a cloth shop when she bought enough material for three house veils at a high price, and I asked her how many veils she needed. Aziza used this expression when she was trying took very authoritarian, and I would suddenly ask something which, had she stopped to answer it in front of the person, it might have broken her aura of authority. The game was to present yourself in full control, whether you were or not. I don't think she had calculated the price of the veils per meter, but had let herself be dwindled without wanting to argue at the risk of being proved wrong.

I was inviting Aziza to Salateen Restaurant in Qessa Khani Bazaar, specializing in Pakistani food. Most women knew the restaurant by name, and regularly ordered from it, but had never been there in person. We went in and shot directly upstairs and to a secluded room with the curtain drawn for privacy from men's glaring eyes. I insisted that she was my guest today, that I could not invite her home as it was not my home, but this was the best I could do. Again, despite her embarrassed lack of knowledge as to what things were, Aziza showed herself very worldly and authoritarian with the waiter. Apparently, I was learning, it was the only way to avoid harassment. If a woman walked meekly in the bazaar, she would get pushed around, but if she walked boldly, aggressively, then she could get by without any trouble.

We ate a grand meal, which she devoured like someone who had been starved in a hostel for a week. Aziza smoked, which greatly pleased me, as I'd so far been the only woman I had seen smoking in this country. But we couldn't get any cigarettes in the restaurant, so I bought two from a street basket on our way out. Here, her impetuosity failed when I asked her if she smoked in the street.

I watched Aziza bargain for a towel, a pair of sneakers, and the veils. At the towel shop, after having passed by and hand-felt a number of identical towels, she began:

"How much is it?"

"Twelve rupees."

Silence.

"How much will you offer?" asked the shopkeeper.

"Eight rupees."

"No, ten is my last price."

"Let's go," she would shove me along. Next, shop, with the same towel:

"How much?"

118

"Thirteen rupees."

"Weeeee! Eight rupees."

"Ten. I won't go lower."

"Eight is my last offer." And she pushed me off hurriedly again, "Let's go." And after we had expired all the towel shops, and she was convinced she knew the right price, she caught my veil and said, "Hang on, I'll go back and get it." And she did, for nine rupees.

Although Aziza claimed it was only her second or third visit to the city bazaar since she had lived in Peshawar, she pushed and pulled me along with tremendous self confidence. She was helping me find some material to make a regular large-size veil for my outings. "These are all Japanese here, expensive and no good. The Pakistani cloth shops are further up." How did she know? But she was right, and we finally found a light blue cotton.

The day was fast closing, and we decided to go back to her family's house, so I could see where it was, in order to return there the next day to work. Across from University Town a dirt road turns off from the shops at Kaka Khel Medicos, and one knows one is in a residential area, with its private air of indignation that does not welcome the stranger. Here, people knew Aziza, and she had to be exceedingly careful to guard her reputation as a good standing, honorable woman. She drew her veil in tighter now than I had seen her do all day in the bazaar or on the buses. This is where her behavior mattered and was observed.

The neighborhood here was almost entirely Afghan. Aziza banged on a wooden door covered over by a dirty white canvas, and we entered. Inside her own home, Aziza was transformed to a meek little girl who served her parents and older brother, and never spoke out of turn. Had it all been a show specially put on for my benefit, or was it the assumed behavior of any dignified woman in the bazaar? In the following years, I discovered it for myself to be the latter. It was time to meet her family and learn more about them.

The family, all separately, had taken twenty days to travel from Kandahar to Quetta, a relatively short distance. They had traveled by bus from one village to another, sometimes held up for days in one spot waiting for transportation to the next village. Aziza's father had broken his hip on the way, and although he has been operated twice, he will remain infirm, with a wooden crutch and walking stick to get around.

Aziza's older brother worked with refugees. An intelligent man, writer and thinker, with very fixed ideas, his left eye couldn't open completely, so that he looked like he was eying you with suspicion. He talked to me about himself: "I got an M.A. from the American University of Beirut, and a doctorate from London. Yes, two degrees, one in economics and one in agriculture. But now I've lost everything, and I don't need all that knowledge any more. It doesn't serve me any purpose here. We owned a lot of farm land around Kandahar, and we've lost everything. What do you want us to do? We can either die or survive now; those are our options. Reporters come to me with such banal questions as concerning my children's education and future. How can we think of such things, like you do in the West, when we are reduced to thinking day to day? Yet we continue to hope that someone will help us, because we are fighting tanks with coca-cola bottles. What kind of war is that?"

Eight months later, another day in the bazaar with Aziza revealed some interesting facts. I had become, with time, a good bargainer. As compared to our first outing in Qessa Khani, since when she had not returned, I no longer followed behind her admiring the feminine superiority she displayed, but this time I led the way. "Wait up," I would hear her from behind. "I can't seem to control my veil and move as fast as you. How do you keep your veil on so tight? It looks like it doesn't give you any trouble." I beamed. Here was someone with a lifetime's experience of wearing veils complimenting the way I handled mine. I also found that I knew all the back alleys and which ones specialized in what wares. I knew about fabrics and prices for hats, for which she now sought my opinion. Most importantly, I drove a harder bargain than she did.

After eating lunch out, Aziza suggested we go to the movies. She had heard there was a good Pashto film, *Shaheed.* Upon entering the cinema, we were at once led to the curtained-off seats in the back by a young boy attempting to flirt with us. "What do you do when a man touches you in public and you're stuck next to him?" I asked her, remembering a situation recently on a bus where I had found myself the only woman, and a man had sat next to me and had harassed me.

"Right away, you turn on him viciously like an animal, and yell at him to keep his hands to himself. He'll be so taken by surprise and ashamed he won't approach you again. But if you just sit there quietly, he thinks you enjoy it, and keeps going."

"I was afraid witnesses might reproach the woman for even addressing the guy."

"No, no. You're obliged to do it. You do it all at once, snapping very harshly and publicly shaming him. He won't come on again. People understand."

I was glad for the information, though I preferred to also keep a knife under my veil to poke at stray hands without launching a verbal scene.

A group of turbaned Afghan youths was seated in the last row of the theater, just in front of the women's section, and as the lights came on at the intermission, one of them, without so much as turning back, grabbed the curtain and swung it shut with a gesture I took as disgust, muttering, "Get those women out of here." The gesture, despite its seeming brutality, was extremely favorably received by Aziza, who smilingly praised the honor and respect for women manifested by the act.

"It's very badly considered, our being here, and everyone would have turned and looked," she explained. "He did it instinctively for our protection." She commended his dignity, adding her belief that only Afghans would act so nobly.

Needless to say, I learned many secrets from Aziza about how to behave appropriately, and her lessons served me well throughout all my years in the NWFP, both in Peshawar and in rural areas.

Pir Baba Shrine

X. PIR BABA – A NIGHT IN THE SHRINE

Gol Jan was a tribal from beyond Gandab in the Mohmand Agency, but he spent his weeks in Peshawar where he ran a successful tea shop in the old city. He was a small man who gave the appearance of a tribal with his plain white head cap and waistcoat. He and his family had sided with the Afghan *mujaheddin* in Afghanistan, and I had once visited his home near Bajawar, in the heart of the Mohmand tribal Agency. But this time, Gol Jan had come to me in Peshawar offering to take me to the most popular shrine near Peshawar, Pir Baba. We would spend the night in the shrine as do thousands of Pashtuns every Thursday, the day of pilgrimages.

Just before we had left my house in Peshawar, I had asked him, "Which veil should I wear, the black or white?" I was asking which would be more appropriate in the religious setting.

"Do you want to go my way or your way?" he asked.

"Yours." I assumed if I let him manage our excursion and behavior, I could perhaps get a better feel for the meaning of the shrine to people, rather than just what it looked like.

"Okay, then put on your full size large black veil, and cover your face entirely so your eyes hardly show. And don't try to talk too much with me on the bus."

I allowed him to take control, and followed him from a few paces behind. We caught a Flying Coach bus from Peshawar directly to Pir Baba. The entire trip, including the horse-drawn cart from my house to the main road, the city bus to the new bus station, and the coach ride, took five hours. Once outside the city, we entered hills filled with giant boulders. I felt Gol Jan to be self-conscious, worried about his position. It reminded me of the young man who had once escorted me from Peshawar up to Sayyed's house in the Khyber area. Occasionally Gol Jan and I would whisper back and forth, but if I even smiled, he would snap at me, "Don't laugh. It looks bad on us both if you do." I knew his concern. If we were suspected of being together but unrelated by family ties, it could mean both of us being arrested.

It was dusk when we reached Pir Baba. I followed Gol Jan through the streets, my vision obscured and frankly blocked by the black surrounding my face. But as we walked, just a little too fast for my liking, I caught the glitter of beads, bangles, eyes, antimony bottles, and women in bright clothes strolling among the stalls showing their faces. I wondered how they could stroll so casually, so dreamily and happily when I had to walk fast and straight, completely covered. I wondered how different the experience might have been had I asked someone from the elite households of Peshawar to come with me instead. I just had my pen and notebook in my hands, and had given my wallet for Gol Jan to put in his pocket.

When we reached the shrine entrance, where there is also a large mosque, the evening prayer had just ended, and an extraordinary rush of men was pouring out. Gol Jan had me sit in a dark corner until it had somewhat subsided, and then signaled to me to follow. Once inside, he announced he had something to do, proceeded to hand me his shoes and told me to go straight to the shrine where he would catch up with me. He went for his ablutions, warning me to walk behind other women at all times and not give the appearance of being alone. I had a slight moment of panic as it was dark and there were so many people, and I thought I would remain alone. I wrapped my veil tightly and advanced through the crowded lanes of beggars, scents, prayer beads, and antimony, attaching myself to other groups of women. But the flow of bodies was strong and aggressive as they were all rushing back to the shrine after prayers.

All around me, from under their blankets, each man seemed to brush his hands along women's body parts, sometimes grabbing what he could. If I stood still for even a moment, they would come and lean against me. I thought at first it was just me, but noticed with relief that every woman around me was being touched and felt in like manner. Here was a context in which hundreds of men and women with no knowledge of each other were thrown together tightly, and suddenly all notions of reserve, shame and respect, so dominant within the home, vanished. I wondered if that was the hidden appeal that this shrine holds for so many Pashtuns of the NWFP. It was extremely uncomfortable, and there was no way to dodge or direct the forceful flow of men as I circled around the shrine.

I noticed a woman clinging to the grate that surrounds the tomb, praying, and she appeared to be left alone, so I went to stand by her, thinking if I looked like I was praying, maybe the men would leave me alone, too. I was standing beside her, clinging to the grate and reciting the sensual sounds of the *kalima,* or Muslim prayer, when Gol Jan finally showed up and led me over to sit on the floor area just beyond the walkway circulating the tomb. Here women and children can sit quietly outside the rush. He showed me a group of women, and told me to sit there. He then circled the shrine once and returned, motioning for me to follow him. This time we circled the shrine from the outside along a dirt terrace, along which families or couples can stroll more quietly, or sit and cling to the grated windows which give onto the women's area. The calm was welcome.

It was here that Gol Jan decided to tell me the story of *Loy Zwan,* a smart boy from a village somewhere whose mother had taught him never to lie. One day he left home to travel, and his mother made him a suit, sewing 5000 rupees into a secret inner pocket. He ran into a band of thieves, who asked if he had any money on him, to which he replied that he had 5000 rupees. They searched him but found nothing, and again asked. Again he told them what he had, again they searched him and found nothing. Three times they asked and searched to no avail, so he opened up the secret pocket and showed them the money, and they asked why he had shown it to them, since they were unable to find it. He answered that his mother had taught him never to lie, and the thieves were so impressed they swore never to steal again, but to follow the right path of Islam.

Gol Jan recounted several such stories he had heard at Friday sermons as we sat on the outer terrace at the shrine windows. A crippled man had followed at a distance and now just sat watching us. Gol Jan was obviously very much on his guard for men wanting to approach me. He knew the shrine tradition far better than I at that point. He walked over and said something to the man, while I remained at the window looking inside, but I couldn't hear what he said.

Instead, I was focused on something going on inside now. Just below the window where I stood looking in, a madman was consumed with praying and chanting, at times yelling out, "Allah!" with ecstasy. To his side were seated an old man and three old women, eating dinner and praying. The old man approached the madman, hand fed him a few morsels of food, then urged him to pray, with hands open. The old man also prayed along with him, looking at him eagerly, crying out, "Pray that God may cure you." Gol Jan had warned me before coming that people at a shrine don't just pray for themselves, but along with and for someone else.

To the other side of the madman was a young boy, lying on a mat separate from his mother and other older women. He was wearing a boy's school uniform and cap, and looked bored. When the old man left the madman, the boy began yelling aggressively to the madman to leave, to get up and go pray around the tomb and heal himself. He threatened to hit the man, raising his voice and hand to him, but the madman stayed put and continued praying. It was an old woman from the first group who again approached the madman, telling the boy to go away, and urging the madman to pray. Her duty finished, she returned to her spot and the young boy came out again, attacking the madman now, yelling at him to get out of there and go circle the tomb. Astonished at this scene, I told Gol Jan, who just laughed, claiming that the boy was only urging him to pray to heal himself, and thus performing a good deed.

My escort was nervously watching some men who seemed to be staring at us. He suggested I go sit inside with the women, so I left the outer terrace and found a spot, unfortunately among a large group of Hindko speakers, so I could neither discuss anything nor explain myself. It was shortly thereafter, while sitting mesmerized by the steady movement of men like water around the shrine, feeling protected on the floor with the women, that I heard Gol Jan's voice again from the window. He was with a policeman, signaling me to the window. I got up to go outside to them, but some angry ladies pulled me back as though I were running away, and led me to the window where the two men were standing.

The policeman began aggressively questioning me: "Do you have someone with you?" I sank, remembering that Gol Jan and I had not agreed as to whom we were to each other for the sake of this trip. I decided to take a path that might lend me some authority, especially as I saw him being led away in the crowd by a policeman.

"Of course," I answered, "he works for me." I've come from my Peshawar office, and brought him to escort me." Still nervous, I demanded, "Who are you, anyway, and where are your papers?" I thought he looked surprised, but he pursued his own interrogation: "What's his name?" I gave the policeman Gol Jan's name, but he just laughed and told me to return to my spot. I knew then something had gone terribly wrong, and we were both in trouble.

I sat down to scan the flowing procession of men for Gol Jan, but I was immediately questioned by all the surrounding women, who repeated my story amongst themselves and to those sitting too far to hear me. I felt contempt from them, like they all accused me of having come here with an unrelated man, obviously in an illicit affair! I felt wrongly accused, horrified and paralyzed at once however, at the thought of the consequences of such an accusation. They then refused me the protection of their midst, but told me to move away and out front to the uncovered floor, on the outskirts, close to the river of men. For a moment I understood the many Pashtun women who had told me over the years of field work that although they resented their current lives, they could never hope to leave the protection that the family offered. They could never hope to find any support in society on their own. I remembered the warnings of a rural mullah who had told me, "Women are respected inside the house. They have no reason to go out, so if they do stray, we no longer have any reason to respect them." I also considered coldly that only miles away across the border in Afghanistan under Taliban rule, I could have been beaten publicly or shot.

The hard concrete floor was filthy, littered with dried chewed-up sugar cane, baby's urine and other like matter. I sat very quietly, focusing on the crowd of men moving through steadily, all their eyes on the seated women. What a place a visual rape! I wanted to go out and enquire about Gol Jan because murmurs around me were that he had been taken to the police station. But I was now seized with fear at the thought of moving alone in this throng of aggressive males, and having to ask someone to show me the way in the dark to the station. A woman approaching a strange man is asking for trouble. So I stayed and asked the women around me instead if they would send their menfolk to the station and plead my case. Gol Jan had returned my wallet with my i.d. earlier, so he had no proof to show for either of us.

A young man finally did come to talk with me, taking all my information and saying he would go do what he could. But by this time, no matter how I tried to convince these women that I was a foreigner, neither Pashtun nor Muslim, they refused to believe me, but shouted, "Don't lie! You're Pashtun and you're going around with an unrelated man.!" I definitely felt excluded from the community, but for the first time it was not on account of being treated as an outsider, but as an insider who had strayed off the narrow path of honor. As an outsider, my blunders were tolerated. As an insider, they were treated as criminal acts, and there was no sympathy or support from this crowd. So I sat quiet. The last thing Gol Jan had whispered to me through the grating had been to sleep here with the women, that he would be outside and that we would head home in the morning.

It was nine or nine-thirty by then, and I felt imprisoned in the shrine. As more groups of women and children settled around me for the night, I was no longer on the outside, but safely surrounded now in my new spot. I sat through most of the night cross legged or with my knees drawn up to my chin on the hard floor. When I couldn't stand it any more, I tried lying down, pushing aside feet, piles of shoes and odd limbs to make sufficient space for my curled up body, still enshrouded in my black veil. It was filthy, but there was no other solution. I no sooner lay my head down that an angry woman yelled at me that she was praying, and that I was taking her space. I sat up again, and another woman handed me a copy of the _Surat-e-Yassin_ and ordered me to pray. And when I took out my notebook to write, I had barely written two words when an angry Pashtun woman demanded to see what I had written. She grabbled my notebook and asked, "It's not the _Qor'an_, is it?" When I confirmed that it wasn't, she took off as abruptly as she had appeared, plodding her heaving feet through the body-covered floor. The first women again reminded me that this was a place to pray and not to write, so I followed her advice and quietly folded everything up inside my veil, lest anyone should try to take it off me. I slipped my wallet down my dress and kept my shoes close by.

I finally did manage to lie down, resting my head on my arm. Twice, I noticed Gol Jan circling the tomb, and we exchanged glances, but could not speak. People were just making sure we kept separate. Men are permitted to sit with their families inside where I was until 11:00 p.m., at which time the police come and order them all away, so that the outskirt of the room, from the shrine circle to the windows giving onto the outside terrace, was left entirely to women and children. From then until dawn, the men can only come inside to circle the tomb and pray. And even that traffic is regulated by law officials. The Police seemed unnecessarily cruel in their approach, hitting people with their guns, terrorizing the crowds and shouting angrily for no reason other than to assert their authority. From where I sat, they appeared to be pinching and grabbing passing women as much as any other men.

The night grew cold: both the concrete under me and the breeze floating in the windows felt icy. Women would walk through this mass of bodies however they could manage, pressing down on heads and other limbs to help balance themselves. We were packed, limbs lying over limbs.

Around 1:00 a.m., a chorus of men's voices began chanting, "*la illaha il-Allah*" (There is no god but Allah). Hundreds of men poured in at one time, though not altering the tempo of the flow around the saint's tomb, their chants deafening. They placed yellow flags around the tomb, circled it, and left. All through the night, the constant movement of bodies around the holy tomb did not let up. I wondered if it was particularly crowded because it was a Thursday, the day of pilgrimage, but I was told it never does lessen, day or night, year after year.

I could only lie down for short periods at a time, and I lay down three times all night. I could hardly call it sleep, because I was so conscious of my body, my hip and shoulder bones pushing against the cold hard, trash-covered concrete. Usually, it was just to relieve my aching sits bones, or to collapse from sheer exhaustion. The night passed in this manner, and before the first light, around 4:30 a.m., I noticed some groups getting up to leave. It was then, when I saw Gol Jan appear in the crowd of circulating men that I motioned toward the door in a plea to leave. He knelt beside me, telling me to cover my face entirely, say nothing, and follow him out. We had a cup of tea and then climbed on a Flying Coach back to Peshawar.

I learned then how Gol Jan had spent his night, and felt terrible that he should have had to succumb to such treatment for being so hospitable towards me. He had been taken to the police station where they had demanded 200 rupees from him before letting him go. He spent the night sitting outside the shrine and circling the tomb every forty minutes to check on me. He had spent some time in the tea house also to keep warm.

Although I was grateful to have experienced the holy shrine to its fullest extent, it had also been one of the more uncomfortable moments of my time in the field.

Ashura Procession in Peshawar

XI. ASHURA IN PESHAWAR

For Shi'ites, this is the height of Islam. "After the month of Muharram," my Iranian friends tell me, "they never speak of Islam again until next year." But the passion and grief that do emerge during these ten days of Muharram, commemorating the martyrdom of the third Imam, Hussein, and particularly on the ninth and tenth day, are something viscerally terrifying. Many Sunites in Pakistan snub it all, and some even tell me that the men involved in the passion play are too doped up on opium to know what they are really doing, or that half of them are not even Shi'ite but are paid to flagellate themselves. It is, once again, one of the misconceptions that circulate among non-participants as a means to disqualify them. But it takes more than money to produce the blood and self flagellation, to produce a man killing himself from flailing his chest violently an entire day. Needless to say, the hostility between Shi'ites and Sunites is felt profoundly in this area, especially in the tribal area of Tirah, where heavy fighting between the two often made the news during my stay in Pakistan.

It was agreed I would go to the two-day celebration of Ashura with some Iranian friends, students I had met from the University of Peshawar. They had advised me to wear my Iranian chador, a black floor-length veil without a face flap like the Pakistani or Afghan veil, in order not to draw attention to myself in the crowd with them. I was glad to have gone with them rather than alone or with Pakistani friends on this occasion.

When we reached the main square of the Sadr Bazaar on the ninth of Moharram, it seemed like all of Peshawar was there, assembled, listening quietly to a man chiding in Urdu over a speaker system about Islam and Pakistan. We climbed to the roof of the Taj Hotel for a better view, and

131

found we were not alone. Every rooftop of the city was occupied, some by women and children, others by young boys, still others by adult men. It was the most panoramic view I had seen of Peshawar yet, although we were only on the third floor. The square seemed tiny, and I was surprised to see how few people were actually there, and how quiet it was.

In their ill-fitting khaki uniforms, and loaded guns pointed at the crowd, the police were omnipresent, constituting a major element of the crowd. The police here often emerge from the lower class, are not highly educated, and seem to derive particular pleasure from roughing up and playing rank on those like themselves, in this case harmless citizens who happened to find themselves in the middle of the road. The Pakistani police resembles a child who is told to watch over a younger sibling and who discovers in that infant a perfect scapegoat for his own wrong doings. The poorer and older these victims, the more they are mistreated. And the solution learned by these helpless victims, is to give in by fear, or to hand out a bribe to get by, and believe they've succeeded in something other than enable a corrupt system to continue.

Today the police feared an uprising at the Ashura manifestations. When religion and politics are so closely affiliated and a people are in an excessively fanatical religious frenzy, it can turn by mere instigation of one or two leaders, into a mass political voice. In Iran also, Ashura is a time of terrific political unrest and mass demonstration, although my Iranian friends informed me that the celebration was mild in Iran as compared to Pakistan. I was finding things very controlled so far.

At intervals during the heated diatribe, unanimous slogans were shouted, and the crowd dispersed. Two circles, one of men and the other of boys, began flogging their backs in steady rhythm, with chains. These also were broken up by police, who feared any sort of passion. They recognized that a man ready to flagellate himself and physically impale himself thus would defy anything and would stand up to any harm threatening from outside, without care. Martial law can only exist as long as people fear for their lives and if, for any reason, the people abandon this fear, then the authorities turn scared. To avoid this, they must regulate the passion and maintain control of the mass's fear.

From the square, we proceeded with the crowds to the husseinyeh, also in Sadr Bazaar. It was mobbed with men and women, separated by a curtain. A first procession of men broke in slowly, slapping their bare chests to blood, some with one hand, other enthusiasts with both, in rhythm as the crowd yelled, "Ya, Hussein! Ya Hussein!" Although it was October, it was still very hot in the Peshawar Valley. I was swimming dizzily in the smell of human blood and sweat, in the sight of glazed eyes, in the aura of delirium. Other non-participant spectators appeared entertained, bemused by the passion play, the living drama of Shi'ite Muslims.

The following morning was the tenth, the height of the entire event. I met up with my Iranian friends and we arrived very early in the old city. It was already crowded with people standing about idly, already selecting their spots from where to watch the procession. Every rooftop of the old city was occupied by a group of silently crouched lamenters, leaning over to see whatever they could. The air was filled with a sense of expectation, but not a frenzied or excited one. The streets and rooftops were for the men, the house interiors for the women who filled every wooden balcony and peered from behind every wooden latticed window.

We idled through the bazaar nibbling dried tamarisk fruit, through the milk and dairy lanes, winding pleasantly through to pass time. My Iranian friends, and I with them, were left alone to wander, and were actually shown right to the procession's starting place. A Shi'ite resident, overhearing us speak Persian, had ushered us through the alley, and ordered me up into his house with the women. Delighted, for it was my first invitation into one of the old city's wooden houses, I climbed straight up to the roof for a view into the surrounding houses as well. But the rooftops were reserved for men; it was clearly not my place, unfortunately.

In the main room of the house, a group of women were huddled over each other, leaning over the pane less wooden window frames. There were few, if any, glass panes in the old city: wood shutters are drawn against the cold in winter. The older women were weeping, younger ones just rocking back and forth, staring ahead with expressionless gazes. A spot was made for me by the window, so I waited, like the others, in silence, while our noses were filled with smoke of aloe burning on braziers in the alley below, and our ears with the Imam's voice echoing from the mosque speaker up the tiny alley. There, below, the men sat on their heels or stood against the wall also rocking in silent anguished mourning. Thousands of people were waiting, moaning, rocking, listening. I had never seen such a large crowd so silent, so docile, unified by agony.

Suddenly two banners, each covered with bright scarves and the hand of Hussein, emerged into the alley from a tiny mosque, followed by a white horse laden down with ribbons, scarves, cloths, and flowers of all colors. He was led up and down the narrow alley, from one mosque into the next, and finally into the street, where the procession began with a first group of self flagellators. Two circles of chanters were formed, beating their breasts in rhythm and forming the center of the procession. "Ya Hussein! Ya Hussein!" would chant one, and the other would answer "Avzela! Avzela! (Farewell!)" They would chant rhythmically and beat themselves as they progressed through the bazaar, stopping occasionally to beat and sing harder, while bare backed ones would strike themselves with chains and razor-blade-covered balls.

After a good portion of the day in this room, I made my way back down into the street and joined my friends. As the procession made its way through the crowd, spectators pushed and strained to see their raw, eaten backs, their glazed, dilated eyes, and their blood dripping to the pavement. Iranians freely followed the procession, but the millions of spectators standing on either side of the streets were held back by chained lines of policemen with canes, rifles, and tear gas in hand. Reaching the end of Qessa Khani Bazaar, we decided we had had enough, and slowly made our way back down the main street, stopping here and there. All the shops were open, and street vendors as busy as ever, impervious to the passion of Ashura. For them, this was not even a Friday, the Muslim day of rest and prayer.

Village of Teri

XII. AFGHAN TENANT FARMERS

Teri had once been a state, just like Dir, Swat and Chitral, which began in the seventeenth century and survived through Partition. It dissolved as a state in 1935, however. Teri village had been the administrative center of the large state which covered most of present day Karak District, including as far as Togh, Hangu, Kohat and Khoshalgargh. It was ruled by a Nawab, but today the nawabship no longer exists. The Nawab, a hereditary post held since the creation of the state, is now an unrecognized figure politically, although he and his household are still held in esteem in Teri. The village today is a long-forgotten hamlet with nothing to attract non-residents, and not even a proper road.

Most people in the NWFP have never heard of Teri. Built up on a hill in a dry desert area, it is camouflaged into the golden brown with its houses of mud and dried mud brick. And although it is just some ten miles off the main Kohat-Banu road, the river prevents access by anything but a reliable off-terrain vehicle, and even these are obliged to work only on their respective sides of the river when the rains render the passage impossible. Passengers are then obliged to cross the river on foot and then catch the transfer vehicle.

Before Partition, this Khattak region was an important Hindu settlement. The Hindus of the area had collaborated with the British, which is how Teri had become a main center of British operations. Vestiges of the Hindu culture can still be seen in the wood lattice balconies, windows and shop doors, in drifting echoes of women pounding laundry with sticks in the river bed below the village, in the sight of unveiled women walking freely with clay pots of water or dry grass bundles balanced on their heads. It is a region rich in peanuts and a dry reed-like grass used to make brooms, baskets, and the cots found throughout Pakistan. The earth, despite its arid appearance, is rich, allowing a small industry of clay pots used for water in most houses of rural NWFP where, even if there is a shared pump, it is only turned on once a day.

Not far from Teri was Ahmadi Banda, where the Salar Mohammad Aslan had first introduced me to Jahanzeb Khan, the commissioner and feudal lord of Teri. In a chauffeured pick-up with three armed escorts, Jahanzeb had come to get me in Ahmadi Banda where I was visiting in 1983, and invite me to visit Teri. I was given a grand tour of the hillside village, and its surrounding lands, all of which seemed to belong to my host, all lived on and cultivated by people working for him who treated him with obsequious servility. At every house we stopped to visit, there was an embarrassed silence until I insisted to be brought inside with the women. As I'd leave the men, I could hear them begin to talk, and I, too, could go chat at ease without having to speak and be spoken to through my host's intermediary.

After visiting and drinking tea in a few surrounding hamlets, our final drive stretched through more hilly, river-crossing, crater-filled tracks to Jahanzeb's wheat fields, turned over to an Afghan refugee family from Khost, Paktia, who worked the land as share-croppers. This time there was no hesitation. Our driver stopped at a distance, so as not to infringe upon the farm's privacy, while Jahanzeb and I walked along the narrow mounded strips of earth delimitating one field from another, to the farm where, without a word, we parted. I walked straight to the encampment, where I remained two weeks, and returned many times in the months and years that followed.

The farm was called Mesheqwali. It was occupied by a large extended family, and I was staying in the house of Mir Ahmad Khan and his wife, Mana, a one-room mud structure with a stove and two rope cots. Mir Ahmad Khan was not the eldest of the clan by age, but in his role as decision maker for the group. Despite his humbling posture and movements, and his soft-spoken matter, he had the powerful gaze of a leader. During the days I lived on the farm, how many times, during our walks through the surrounding hills, he would turn and, with his turban resting over his eyebrows, and his deep commanding eyes and thinly cut face, would look me in the eyes to correct me on a point or convince me of his viewpoint. I felt at ease there because the hospitality was not forced for the sake of impressing the neighbors, and I was not obliged to play the fool in order to break down walls of formality and be permitted to participate in chores and activities. Finally, I was not confined to a walled-in courtyard, but could walk, be alone, work in the fields or the house. Most alluring was that I could be at ease with the men as well as the women, without causing suspicion in everyone's imagination.

One is never alone around Afghans, though the game is to make one believe one is. One day when I was sitting in the sun with the women watching Mana embroider flowers on her father's blanket, and listening to two of her sisters-in-law tell their life story, Mir Ahmad Khan approached our group, but kept his distance and did not attempt to interrupt us. The men were squatted at a distance in the shade of some trees, while we were just outside his hut, but this was not his territory. A man does not intrude on a women's assembly. So he stood sternly outside our circle and ordered a child to bring him his shoes. But his mere presence had broken the magic of our assembly, and when he was certain our discussion had died, he was able to address me. He announced that if I wanted to take a walk, I could go in any direction I wanted. I was free. I had earlier expressed that the most difficult part for me about living in this country was to be surrounded by beautiful country I did not feel free to walk around in. I have always been an outdoors person and a hiker. So, this statement came like a gift from heaven. I had waited five months to be told I could go walk where I wanted, alone, and I lost no time. Not too far away, perched on a small hill in the shade of a low tree, I sat down to go over some notes, feeling the relaxation of a complete linguistic release. The Paktia dialect was new and difficult for me, and kept my head working hard every waking moment, so the break would help me renew the attack with fresh initiative.

There was not a sound, which was strange in this desert hilly area, where the slightest noise carries at least seven or eight miles. Presently, I heard a spit and footsteps that sounded near. But when I looked up, attentive as a hunter, or the prey rather, I saw in the distance a man walking leisurely along the dusty path alone, steady in his pace, looking to none of the six directions of his universe. His white turban tail waved against the golden blond desert colors. We greeted each other as he drew near and I recognized him as a young boy from the farm, chasing partridges. He had a sling, but was mostly checking his traps dug in the ground, expressing disappointment that they all seemed empty that day. The area was littered with partridge traps.

We were soon joined by Khan Mahmad, one of Mir Ahmad's brother's from the farm, and the three of us sat a moment in silence, just gazing out

139

to the plains in the late afternoon sun. Khan Mahmad was holding in one hand, as they all do here, a small quail, training its legs for the fights by bouncing them on his palm. It was a sight I had become accustomed do. Every man from this farm held a quail in his hand at all times, exercising its legs out in the open or hidden in the dark warmth under his shawl. The result was they consistently took home the winnings at the bird fights in Teri.

"Have you gotten lost?" asked Khan Mahmad. "Will you come back for tea?"

Every day I was there, I took an hour or two to myself to go walk in the hills, but each time, I ended up followed by someone from the farm, guarding me casually from a distance. I didn't always see them, but could hear footsteps in the loose stones, or a whistle. I knew that whoever it was knew exactly where I was but wouldn't approach me directly. As Mir Ahmad had expressed to me, "You are my responsibility. I'd have to pay the ransom money if you were kidnapped. I'd do pashto or kill myself." I had heard almost everyday since first arriving in the NWFP of the dangers to foreigners, especially women: "There are bandits all over, especially in and close to the tribal hills. When they spot a woman alone, they know she's worth a great deal, so they kidnap her and sell her to Arabs, or just hold her for ransom." Real or imagined, it was a real fear in every Pashtun's thinking, so I just smiled at the thought of my distant watchmen, and enjoyed my precious moments of near privacy. We often walked back together.

Once, on a walk home from the hills, we had been running down a pebbly hillside laughing when the guys decided to engage in boulder throwing to see who could throw a heavy rock the farthest. I sat as the judge, musing over the *mujaheddin*, who continually had to prove their strength, their manlihood, to each other and now to me.

Another time I had hiked farther than usual, across the valley and into the next set of higher mountains. I had stopped, perched high to watch the river, the next larger village, and Mana with the other Mesheqwali women, their bright red and purple dresses swinging under the graceful motion imposed by the weight of water pots on their heads. I could hear every sound of life distinctly: shepherds yelling at their herds, women pounding laundry, children playing, a wood flute, a singer, roosters crowing. That day I was being guarded by Mir Ahmad himself, and Mana's younger brother, who caught up with me after a time. In my plastic slippers I kept slipping awkwardly on the loose stones in the steep hills, while they just

140

ran like goats, showing me with proud smiles how they maneuvered in guerilla warfare.

They had an axe with them, and when they spotted a tree stump they decided to cut it. There was ample fire wood at home, and no real need for more, but the stump and the axe were there, and so were we, so they set to hacking. It was very hard wood, and with all their striking, half of it disappeared in scattered chips, which I began to collect in my veil. But Mir Ahmad gently threw them back afterward, laughing, "No need. We were only cutting to pass time." I was stunned. They had put all their energy into battling this rock-hard stump of wood, blistering their hands to blood, and would not give up. There was a moving joy taken in this demonstration of strength, determination and manliness. They would smile casually, gently to me as they took turns with the axe, and I knew they were exerting themselves painfully without wanting to show it. This performance was aimed at physically performing for me what they spent so much time telling me about verbally: their prowess and their fighting ability. It was a show of Afghan character in the current war. They would never complain, never cry out in pain, never give in to weakness. Everything was manifested in the cutting of that tree stump without a single word.

This family, as so many Afghans I encountered exiled inside Pakistan, were so proud to be Afghan, so proud of title of freedom fighter, so proud of the difference between themselves and the Pakistani hosts. Mir Ahmad and the other men on the farm would spend evenings after dinner, bouncing their birds under their blankets and telling me about these differences, always putting everything into a "Khattak versus Afghan" frame. "We will never give our children to them, or take their women. They may speak Pashto, but they are not Pashtuns." The comparisons were endless.

There were over fifty small wicker cages for quail which we covered each night with bright handkerchiefs. At dawn and dusk, these birds make the loudest hue of love calls to each other, so that it was impossible to keep them within the camp. The men would carry them all out and hang them in the wheat fields for the night, but still, before sunrise each morning, their clamor woke me up. I would lie on the bed, my head poking out the small opening in the wall, and in the morning haze, would see each man individually walk out, wrapped in his blanket and holding a small spouted *lota* of water, to some solitary spot where he could squat in privacy and perform his ablutions. It was a tranquilizing sight to wake to, while Mana would already have lit a fire in the small room, and be making tea.

141

In the evening, just before dark, I would set out with two young men, carrying a male and female quail in their cages, and a large net. It was quail hunting time, and we would walk quietly through the fields, I under the charm of the evening light, and tense with eagerness at the hunt. When they thought we had reached a good spot, Sardar would start hissing through his teeth to stir the caged quail to a mating call in response, thus attracting other birds in turn. If any entered the field, we would cast our giant net over the field and catch it, and if unsuccessful, we would return to the camp just as satisfied from the mere joy of the hunt.

On Fridays, naturally, the men would all disappear to Teri with their quails and partridges for the fights, from which they would return quietly triumphant, proudly presenting their wives and mothers with sugar, fruit, or a little meat, which we would set about cooking at once. There was no food conservation to speak of here, or in most homes anywhere in rural NWFP. Only small quantities were ever purchased for immediate consumption, and there was never an abundance of anything, or a single morsel thrown out.

When I was in Mesheqwali in winter, I helped the family pick peanuts. The earth was hard as rock despite the fact that it had been ploughed by a two-cow plough. If you used the hard pick with too much force, you broke the peanuts. At night we would cook the dried peanuts in a deep pan filled with sand for an even heat over the fire.

Mana and I also spent time together preparing meals, walking to the river to fill clay pots with water, milk the cows, and other house-related tasks. When one of the calves died, she gutted it and stuffed it with hay. Then we dragged it in front of the cow and sprinkled water on it to freshen the scent. The idea was that the cow, stimulated by the scent of her calf, would continue to produce milk. Mana said everyone did that.

Once, Mana and I walked across the muddy fields to the road leading to Teri to visit her aunt, Bata. Bata, also related to Mir Ahmad Khan had a slightly different living arrangement. She and her husband had arrived from Khost in 1984, long after Mir Ahmad Khan's family, and had been given a vacant house inside Teri to occupy. Bata considered herself very fortunate not to have to live in the refugee camps. The house was empty because the family had relocated to Karachi, leaving their in-laws next door. This house was like many in the NWFP, inhabited only by women because the men were all in Saudi Arabia working. So they had built a wall between the two houses and let the Afghans live in the empty one. In exchange, the Afghans cut wood for them, gave them milk from their cow, fetched water for them, and went to get the doctor when they needed him. In short, they provided a traditional male role in lieu of paying rent. Bata spoke very favorably of her Pakistani neighbors. "My own relatives in Mesheqwali didn't help us out as much when we arrived empty-handed. We had no clothes, no bedding, no utensils, nothing. We had left suddenly because of all the bombs."

I was unable to spend extended periods of time in Mesheqwali in 1986, when I had my daughter, Lawangina, with me. The exposure to fleas, malaria, and the doubtful river water for drinking were things I didn't mind for myself, but could not subject a baby to. So, I put in day visits when residing in nearby Ahmadi Banda. But the farm in Mesheqwali always stayed in my mind a spot where I had found some tranquility and ease, and from where I had been able to enjoy the desert mountains my own way.

'Ali Heydar, Poet

XIII. RAISSA, AFGHAN WAR WIDOW

I had met Amin and Bahadar Shah in Swat where they had come with their families to escape the oppressive summer heat of Peshawar in 1987. Now they were back in the refugee camp of Jalozay, outside Peshawar, and I had gone for a visit. They were from an educated, upper middle class family in Kabul, with root origins in Zuruk on the father's side, and Panjshir on one of the mothers' sides. They had crossed over as a group of sixty when the war first broke out, by way of Zuruk and Parachinar. They had been among the first to settle in Jalozay Camp in the early 80s, when there were only a few houses and no transportation to Peshawar. They had built an elaborate compound for the entire extended family, according to rules as to who participates in what and for which reasons.

At first, most of my conversations were with Bahadar Shah, who was Amin's paternal cousin, married to his sister. His own parents and brothers were still in Kabul, explaining why he and his sister were with his wife's family. Bahadar Shah was following a paramedic course for refugees taught by a German NGO. He had been a student in the Law College at the University of Kabul prior to the Soviet invasion. He was very involved in the war, and intended to use his medical knowledge to help his country.

The other person I talked with and spent the night with in this household was Raissa, married to the oldest son in this family. Her husband had been in Dubai for eight years, coming home occasionally on leave and sending gifts for his epileptic daughter. Raissa and her children occupied the nicest room of the compound, with a private verandah, bathroom, garden, and water faucet. She ate separately with her children in her own quarters, sign of an independent household, even though she worked and cooked over in the central house and kitchen.

Raissa's own family had remained in Kabul, and in the absence of her family and husband, her brothers-in-law had urged her at first to work in the *jihad*, or holy war against the Soviets. She confessed to me that she did it primarily as a way to visit her own family. She had returned home inside Afghanistan three times thus far, but her in-laws had caught on to her and would not let her return now. Her only desire now was to leave and go live with her sister in Los Angeles.

Like many women *mujaheddin*, Raissa took her children inside Afghanistan with her all three times. Once inside Kabul, she would work for the Russians during the day. Then at night she would circulate from house to house informing the *mujaheddin* as to what the Russians were doing.

What amazed me in Bahadar Shah's and Raissa's accounts were their descriptions of the Russians as negligent fools, vulnerable by their unawareness of what passed right under their noses. Raissa claimed that many women could do the open spying she had done due to the Russian negligence. Apparently they smoked a lot of hashish and drank a lot of vodka, and were often unaware. Bahadar Shah had driven a taxi in Kabul and told a story of being stopped by two drunk Soviet soldiers one night who asked him in broken Persian, "Which is better, the Russian or the American car?" He answered, "The Russian, of course!" So, they asked, "Who are better people, Russians or Americans?" "Russians, indeed!" he replied. So they congratulated him, climbed into his cab, and invited him to drink with them in an officers' club.

When I asked more about the women's involvement in the *jihad*, Raissa began to describe a center in Peshawar where women assembled to talk, lecture, politicize and plan missions, but Bahadar Shah interrupted her sharply and then explained gently to me that it was something they didn't want any foreigners involved in, for fear of Russian spies. It was not at all open, and few people even knew about it.

Conversations with Afghan refugees over the years, whether in camps in Pakistan or in U.S. cities, revealed that perhaps one of the most difficult and degrading things about being a resettled refugee is coping with the loss of class distinction. It is something I have seen time and again with economically secure Afghans who have found their way to American cities. Former doctors or highly positioned government officials are reduced to positions and incomes of night watchmen, street venders, taxi drivers and theater ticket collectors, with their wives working as cooks and maids for others in order to allow the kids to go to school. Such a jump in class is a humiliating experience for anyone to go through, and even more so when one comes from an intensely class conscious society.

Amin, Bahadar's sister's husband, and his family, were an educated mid- to upper class Kabul family. In the camp, they were thrown in among people they considered far below them, nomads. They regarded themselves as alienated within the camp, and desperately wanted to move out. Amin even spoke of moving back to Afghanistan despite the war, to escape the indignities of the camp.

One major way in which they differed was in their dress. As I looked through the family album, I saw some of the women, like Raissa, dressed in Western clothes in Kabul. In the refugee camps, they all wore Pakistani-style pants and dresses with light chiffon head veils. This had caused them immediate problems at the public water faucets in the camp. When they had gone at first, the other more rural and traditional women had insulted them for their shameless clothing, and chased them away. Amin had, through some connections, managed to obtain a water line to his compound, so they didn't have to use the public faucets. The camp had tanks with faucets located at points so that up to six compounds depended on any one tank, but now Amin, and one other household that he knew of, had their own pipes.

I had often participated in discussions by both Pakistanis and Afghans concerning the implications of dress, especially for women. The two were always discernable in public by their dress. Afghan men wore turbans, beards, waistcoats and hats. Afghan women wore a fuller dress than their Pakistani counterpart, and richer colors. If not wearing traditional *kuchi*, or nomad attire, then their trousers tended to be white with a lace hem at the bottom, as opposed to the Pakistani style of matching dress and trousers. And the Afghan *burqa*s had tighter pleats. I was familiar with most regional dialects by now, and could tell pretty nearly where any Pashtun came from based on their dress and speech. I had often heard from *kuchi*s that the greatest difficulty of being exiled in Pakistan for them was the issue of dress. For them, it was crucial to their identity to maintain their heavy, thick dress, constituting about fifteen meters of material, including both the dress and trousers. A Pakistani woman's suit used only five meters, and very light fabrics. The heavy suits were fine in Afghanistan where the weather was cool and the cloth inexpensive. But here it was not only a tremendous expense, but unbearable in the heat. Some younger refugee girls raised in Pakistan were now beginning to wear lighter clothes and even Pakistani suits on occasion.

This was what Raissa faced at the camp well. Afghans in Pakistan had a tendency to distinguish themselves from Pakistanis by their firm hold on honor. My friend, Aziza, had adamantly claimed that Pakistani men did not respect women like Afghan men did. Hence, dress symbolized not only ethnic identity but an outward performance of Afghan honor in face of the infidel Russian and the abusive Pakistani. Light dress was considered shameless for women. When I suggested Raissa was lucky her husband had not made her change to be like other women in the camp, she agreed: "Of course!. He took my side and separated for my sake, and I still wear my own type of clothes."

This family was alienated from most others living in Jalozay Camp. Amin explained that they had no friends there, and that they were snubbed by everyone. "They reject our clothes; they reject the fact that we wash our hands with soap; they reject the fact that we change our clothes and bathe every two to three days, if not more often."

The family had invited me and my daughter for one of their children's first birthday party. For weeks, everyone had talked about nothing else, insisting that I must come. Bahadar had gone to Thall to escort an aunt to Peshawar for the occasion, and he had come to get me also. After the party, however, held on a Friday, Bahadar had expressed his opinion to me: "It was a mistake. We never should have done it, but the others insisted. Celebrating birthdays is strictly a European or inner Kabul tradition. I understand their desire to do it, but they should have kept it hidden. Instead, they invited all the neighbors in the camp and made a big show of it. The household across the alley from us has lost four men this week. Everyone in this camp has lost people and is mourning. They live in sadness and we celebrate the joy of a child's birthday! People look down very hard on this. Since the war, even weddings have taken place in silence, with minimum celebration."

After staying with Raissa in the camp, and returning several times for weekend visits, Raissa and Bahadar Shah especially opened up to me. I was spending a few days as Raissa's guest, when Bahadar Shah came in one night and very quietly talked with me. I had mentioned that I felt like I was receiving the cold shoulder from some other women in the compound, particularly the baby's young mother, who had celebrated his first birthday. She seemed to find every occasion to criticize the way

I raised my daughter, and had not let me have any fresh cow's milk in the morning to feed Lawangina, claiming it was for her own son. She seemed to be going out of her way to make me feel unwelcome. Bahadar now addressed this issue with me, trying to explain the situation. The fact that I was Raissa's guest had made the rest of the family turn against me and treat me as they did her. Bahadar exposed the power structure of the household, and how it had changed since they had moved here, and how they had turned Raissa, an upper class educated woman, into a servant with unfed, neglected, and uneducated children. Bahadar went on to praise Raissa, pointing out that she, more than all the others, helped me out with Lawangina when I came to visit.

He then began exposing Raissa's story. She had nothing, not a dime. Her husband had been away now for eight years. Apparently, he earned and saved money, and was sending it in secret to his mother and brothers, with instructions not to give any to his wife. She had no allowance to purchase things for her children; no proper foods, no medical treatment. If she asked for anything, she was told she had no rights in this household. She was to work for them, eat the food given her, and otherwise keep to herself. Bahadar sympathized with Raissa, seeing himself as an outsider also, as he was a paternal cousin and married to one of the family sisters. He claimed the brothers had specifically told him, too, that he should appreciate the food he received, but that he should not try to oppose the family in any way or they would fight him. He continued in detail: "Raissa is kept here as a slave. She does most of the house work, and if ever she's caught idle with her kids, they all get on her back. She does all the washing, feeding, cleaning of the cows, but gets no milk for her three year old sickly son or her epileptic daughter. So you can understand why you, as her guest, are treated as she is."

The reason for the shift in status and the fall of Raissa and so many like her was that her husband was not supportive of her. This was a prime example of how a woman could be made or broken by her husband. Her mother-in-law was trying to find another wife over Raissa for her son, which would mean the end of Raissa, who held little hope for herself and regarded her life as finished. She had also abandoned any hope for her daughter, a young adolescent now, kept as a slave without education. She could offer little more for her son's future, either. Bahadar explained, "If they keep Raissa and her children suppressed and ignorant, then they, particularly her son, will never grow to a position where he could avenge his mother or fight for his own rights. They thus create a dependence of these people on themselves. They create live-in servants - no, slaves, because they are not paid."

With her high level of education, Raissa had been offered a job teaching in the camp girls' school. It would have paid her over $100.a month for herself and her children. But her in-laws had refused to allow her to take it, threatening that if she ever left the compound they would not permit her to return. This rule also applied to walking her three-year old son to pre-school. "He's too young to go by himself," said Raissa, "and the other boys won't look after him."

I asked why, despite these circumstances, Raissa lived in the nicest house in the compound. Bahadar explained that when they had first arrived, they were still a close family and she was the respected oldest daughter-in-law. Then, as her husband left her, his family also turned against her. I was beginning to understand the impact of what few women had dared to answer when I asked them who a woman's greatest enemy is. "Her husband. He can ruin her as well as he can make her a queen." Raissa, like most women in her position, felt helplessly locked into her slot. There was no ready-made way out for her, and an entire society against her if she tried to break out. The last time Raissa had been to Kabul for *jihad*, her mother had pleaded with her to remain, but she had to go back.

I was at first overwhelmed again, as I had been upon hearing so many similar stories, by this innate sense of duty on behalf of women toward their husband's families. Was it duty, or fear? And then I thought of the camp I had visited for Afghan war widows, for those women turned out by their in-laws, often without their children, after their husbands had died or disappeared and the family no longer could keep the extra mouth to feed. Probably in that camp I had experienced the greatest feeling of total loss and despair ever. These women, completely without any male relatives, were now at the complete mercy of whatever would be provided for them by the state. We have all read about their plight at some point or other. So, was Raissa better off being allowed to remain where she was, despite the conditions, and keep her children? Once again, it screamed out: "Live by the rules of what your society demands, or lose your society." Rejection is a heavy price to pay in Afghan society.

Carrying water

XIV JAHANGIR FALLS IN LOVE

I met Jahangir and his family through some friends who knew them, and we all spent Christmas at their house in Quetta. Jahangir lived with his parents and two other brothers, with their wives and children, in a compound in an area of Quetta known for its community of *mohajers*, or Afghans settled there before the Soviet invasion. Most of the community was Shi'ite, Dari-speaking, migrated from Kandahar and other parts of Afghanistan. Jahangir's mother was Russian, his father a Tajik from northern Afghanistan.

The following is Jahangir's own account of an obsession he had had before being married. He told it one night when a group of us were exchanging personal stories.

One day, when Jahangir was about eighteen years old, he was walking home from school through the mud lanes of the Afghan district of Quetta for lunch. He was surprised to find the door to his house locked, and no one to answer his knocks and calls. That night, his mother explained that she had been out at her friend's house helping her to prepare her daughter's wedding chest. "I'll be there again tomorrow, so go there for lunch."

The next day, Jahangir went to the house, knocked at the door and backed away a step or two. Just then, a beggar came down the alley cantillating the usual Thursday plea for alms so that the people of the house, having heard his voice from inside, assumed the knock had also been his, and opened the door. From behind it appeared a girl clothed in the black veil worn in Iran, and here by Hazara Shi'ites. Her sleeves were rolled up, her face an alabaster white, eyes jet black, brows dark and arched high on her forehead.

Jahangir dumbly stared at her, who, unconscious of his presence across the alley, poured a small vessel of flour into the beggar's bowl. Suddenly her glance fell on Jahangir, and she slammed the door shut at once, flush at having been espied unawares by a stranger. He was still standing there, stunned by the shock of the slam after being so entranced by this beatific vision, when the door very slowly opened again, revealing first a hand, then one eye, and both, until she stood plainly visible before him and to him. Quite unaware of his own movements, Jahangir took the front of his long shirt in both hands and held it up in front of him in a begging gesture. He had not moved forward from his position several steps away from the door, and the black-eyed girl reached out her arm and emptied the last remaining grains of flour into the mud alley. Symbolically, Jahangir gathered up his shirt as though it had been filled, and remained staring at the girl, who now closed the door quietly.

Waking jerkily from his dream, Jahangir remembered that his mother was in this house, and again he knocked. Again, the same girl answered, but this time it was official, and, quite veiled, she showed him to the men's guest room, where his mother brought him some lunch. He was still dazed. "Eat!" his mother urged him.

"Uh-huh," he answered pensively without reacting.

"Eat!", she ordered, a little more convincingly.

A week later Jahangir became ill and was taken to the hospital to have his tonsils removed. One day his mother came to visit, and with her was another female figure, hidden beneath her black Shi'ite veil. Jahangir could not see the girl, but like most men in this part of the world, he had learned to recognize women by a foot that might show, the shape of the head, or the curves of the veil, and he immediately guessed it was the girl of his obsessions. His mother gave him a magazine, but he snubbed it saying he would prefer a book. "Anyway," he added, "where did you get a magazine? We don't have any in the house."

His mother casually, without turning her head, motioned behind her to the black silent figure. "Oh, it's just that woman's daughter. She figured with you sick in the hospital, you might enjoy a magazine."

Jahangir eagerly took up the magazine and tucked it under the blanket on his chest, gripping it tightly with both hands and wishing they would leave. And when they did, of course, he leafed through it carefully, looking for a message from her. There was indeed a poem, inscribed on a page. He wrote one in reply underneath hers, and sent the magazine through his brother back to the girl with many thanks. The same magazine went back and forth several times between the hospital and the girl's house.

Jahangir's secret love affair lasted ardently for five years, with only his mother and the girl's mother knowing about it. His own mother, being originally Russian and Christian, sympathized with her son and did all in her power to obtain the girl for him in marriage. But despite all their pleas and cries, the girl was not given up. She was from a Shi'ite family, and Jahangir could not convert from his Sunite faith and expect to remain in the bosom of his own family. It tore him apart the day he learned she was to be married to someone else.

Today, Jahangir is unaware if the girl is alive, if she still lives in Quetta or has been moved to a farther place, if she still remembers him and nourishes the same fire for him as he does for her. He spent some ten years in solitude before accepting to marry a woman proposed by his mother to cure his melancholy. He has been a good husband and a loving father since then.

When Jahangir finished his story, told in the presence of his own wife who sat there quietly with a baby on her lap and another one at her side, he addressed her, saying, "You really are quite a woman." Her only response was a sigh and the glimmer of a tear. "That's what life is about: what happened to me, and what happened to you, and then being able to talk about it."

XV. CELEBRATING PERSONAL EVENTS

My thirtieth birthday in 1986 was an exciting event in my own life, and I thought it worth celebrating, but I also used it as an occasion to put myself to a test and celebrate the way rural Pashtuns celebrate events of joy. I was living in Madyan at the time, renting the small annex to a larger house belonging to my friend, Moambar, whom I had known since 1979. The house was located far above the main village, with no access but a steep path up the mountain. The family had moved out of the village and up here for privacy since I had first known them. I was good friends with the women of his house: Moambar's mother, wife, and three sisters-in-law.

I had invited some twenty households for the party, families with whom I had worked and developed a relationship over the past six months, from local religious families to lower class entertainer families and Afghan refugees. The main difficulty was in not having a house or household support large enough to pull off what I engaged in. I had bought all my supplies and had asked various people in the village to help me by cooking large quantities.

The day began at 5 a.m., when Mina, my nanny, began fixing tea and showering. Shortly afterward, she left to see about the meat, of which we had ordered ten kilos the day before. She and Umar, a young man from the village whom I employed to transcribe my tapes, returned with the meat, and Mina put some water on to heat, insisting I shower, wash my hair and put on clean clothes for the occasion. I slunk into the smelly outhouse to wash for the first time in days. Needless to say, washing was an ordeal and not a priority in our daily lives. Mina, who was dark-skinned and had a great sense of humor, yelled to me, "Scrub your neck and ears white like mine!" I could hear her and Umar laughing, but the message was that I had become rather dirty. I had not seen myself in a mirror in weeks.

Then the work began. Umar and I went to the Afghan homes where one was cooking fifteen kilos of rice, and the other two kilos of meat. We had supplied them with all necessities for this, including the tomatoes, onions, salt, wood, and fat. Until everything was actually ready I was running around bringing and getting things, nursing Lawangina, and pouring juice for the guests as they began to come. Many children showed up, but only seventeen adults, not including the eight from my and Moambar's houses. Moambar had offered me the use of his courtyard and the help of his women to receive the guests, as mine was not enclosed, and too small to accommodate the large numbers. Pahlawan, Moambar's brother-in-law, came with me to carry two huge pots of rice up the mountain, while Umar went to get the pot of meat from the Afghans. This was where I made my first mistake. I had them lay the pots down in the empty guest room of my house, separate from the main house with the guests. There, we began filling the trays with rice - a bowl of meat and sauce atop each one - and Moambar carried them in to the groups of assembled women.

One woman claimed she was fasting that day, and asked to be given her portion to bring home. I agreed. I wanted to send a tray to each of the houses where they had cooked the meat and rice, so these were prepared and sent out with Umar, leaving Pahlawan in my guestroom with the pots. On my way back to the house at one point, I noticed a woman leaving with a large pot wrapped in a kerchief. I asked where she was headed and she answered, "To my sister's mother-in-law." And who had given her the meat? Her sister. I let her go, but was furious. I could do nothing; the harm had been done. People had started sending large trays home, as well as to relatives' houses. When I had left, one entire pot of rice was left, and half the meat, but when I returned, Moambar and Pahlawan looked at me in surprise, exclaiming that there was nothing left, only enough for the four women of the house who had not yet eaten.

I later discovered what had occurred during my brief absence, as far as the pots, anyway. The man helping out had heaped a tray of meat, hidden under a pile of rice, and had taken it home. Moambar's wife had prepared a pot full of meat and rice to send to her daughter in-law's (the woman I had seen leaving) house. And another guest had had her children bring a tray back to her house.

Had one more guest arrived, I would have sunk with shame, because there was nothing left. Later on, everyone was eager to enlighten me as to their version of what had gone wrong inside the main house. Even though the groups eat communally by hand off the trays, in each bowl is a spoon with which one serves one's self and the others with meat and sauce on their portion on rice. The four sisters-in-law of Moambar's house were situated so that one sat in each group of guests, responsible for washing the women's hands, bringing water, and dishing out the meat. Someone later told me that they had given the biggest, choicest bits to their own children and family, giving the Afghans and other village guests the bones and a little sauce. Someone else told me that one of the sisters had taken the water melons to cut inside her own room, having all the household children eat large center chunks as fast as she could cut them, while a few trays of thin slivers were sent out to the Afghans and others villagers.

Throughout the entire afternoon, until late that night, individuals came and complained that they had eaten nothing but a morsel, that so-and-so had stolen everything. A dispute broke out between Mina and Moambar's wife, who accused Mina of stealing melons. Mina defended herself, claiming they were for the folks who had received no rice because Moambar's wife had stolen it all. Then Mina went to Moamabar's brother-in-law's house to beg a little rice for Lawangina's dinner, as we had not prepared another meal.

The event had proved a fiasco, showing me how little I understood about managing food distribution, and how easily I had been taken advantage of and then blamed for the blatant mismanagement.

Not even six months later, I decided to attempt the ordeal again, this time to celebrate Christmas, this time in another village where I was living, Ahmadi Banda. This time, rather than invite guests to my house, I had purchased a young goat, and had arranged to have someone come slaughter and butcher it outside my house so that I could package portions of meat inside newspaper and distribute it to friends and acquaintances throughout the village. This form of gift-sending without actually inviting large numbers to one's house is often practiced among Pashtuns. A number of young girls assisted me in this task

I imagined that by distributing rather than inviting, which was in keeping with local tradition, it would allow me some privacy to enjoy Christmas day with my daughter, something we were rarely able to do.

Although we were always together, we were seldom alone together just to play and I had reserved this day. But the days that followed brought reproach as to how I had handled sharing my Christmas feast.

My neighbor, Jansardara, was furious with me, claiming, "Since when are the organs a share of meat?" She had specifically asked me for the organ meat, which I had packaged as her share, unaware that it was considered an extra and not a proper portion of meat. She harshly reprimanded me: "If I had known you counted them like that, I would never have asked you for them." The worst part was I could have sworn I had sent her a portion of meat apart from the organs. Not only did Jansardara reproach me for having shortchanged her in meat, but she made no mention of the gifts I had offered each member of her family. Once again, however, I was condemned to failure by a lack of household support. I realized I had no means beyond my instructions, to proficiently monitor where my young helpers were actually delivering each portion.

I felt the worst for my friend, Farida, and her family. They were from the large family of mullahs in the village, and extremely close with me since years. Farida had specifically requested the head, and I had inquired at least six times the previous day from different people if the head and feet constituted a full share, and had been assured that it did. So I didn't send them a portion apart. I knew Farida would never tell me, but I was sure she was hurt now, too, probably reporting the injury to others.

By the end of the two-day celebration, I gave up to despair and broke into tears at dinner, feeling I had gone to all this trouble and had pleased no one, and therefore accomplished nothing. There were moments like that when, in private, I felt I could do nothing right. All I had really managed to do was set off arguments and hostilities, alienating myself temporarily from families whose friendship I treasured. That was my last attempt at a large-scale celebration of any kind. My two defeats had made it clear that I was not equipped socially or physically (by the size of my household) to accomplish such a feat.

GLOSSARY

Angrez. A term used generally to identify a foreigner, sometimes specifically a person from England.

Attan. Pashtun national dance.

Bibi. A lady. A title used for a woman.

Burqa. A full body-size pleated veil fitted over the head and down to the feet, leaving a laced portion over the eyes for visibility.

Dem, Dema. A man or woman from a social group in low esteem known as entertainers, musicians, barbers, and midwives.

Gham. Sadness. An event of sadness or loss, such as a funeral.

Gora. Unrefined sugar, hardened into a ball. Cheaper than white powder sugar and commonly used as a sweetener in poor rural areas.

Hujra. A guest room, or house, separate and outside the main house, where male guests can be entertained.

Jerga. A group of elders holding authority. It can range from national assembly to a village group deciding and ruling over disputes.

Jihad. A war or struggle in the name of Islam.

Jinn. Spirits, referring to hysteria or dementia.

Kabab. Skewered meat, usually cooked over coals.

Kala. A fortress, constituting several houses occupied by a single extended family.

Khan. A landlord. Also a title given to someone of Pashtun descent.

Kuchi. A nomad, or semi nomad.

Lota. A common household item, being a spouted vessel used mostly for ablutions and cleansing after a bowel movement.

Muhajer. Refugee.

Mujahed. Someone involved in a *jihad.* During the 1980s, the term was used to identify anyone in the struggle against the Russian invasion.

Walima. A large wedding reception, usually held in a public place, among the wealthy in Peshawar.

About the Author

Benedicte Grima is a trained ethnographer from the University of Pennsylvania who spent over ten years traveling, living and participating in rural life in the border area of Afghanistan and northwestern Pakistan as part of her doctoral research. Four years of extensive language training in Pashto and Farsi at the Institut des Langues Orientales in France, and an M.A. from the University of Paris in Iranian Studies, armed her with the linguistic skills to feel at home among Pashtun men and women ranging from farmers to intellectuals. She has published a book, "The Sorrows Which Have Befallen Me": The Performance of Emotion Among Paxtun Women, and numerous academic articles on various aspects of Pashtun women and culture.

Printed in the United States
122683LV00004B/3/A

9 781420 806748